Read my mind

WHY IS POETRY VITAL FOR CHILDREN?

Fred Sedgwick has a passion for poetry and young poetry-makers, particularly at the primary level. In this, his latest book, he aims to help all those involved with children and their learning through poem-writing improve their practice. He argues that through poetry, children can learn about the whole curriculum, including history and science.

The book begins with an introduction outlining the importance of poetry, and defining it. It discusses poetry in terms of children's learning and the imagination. Case studies are used to show how children learn about themselves – first, their bodies, and second their thoughts and emotions – through the writing of poetry. It then considers how children learn about their environment and the relationship between themselves and their environment. Finally, he discusses his techniques for getting children to write and provides recommendations for further reading.

Fred Sedgwick is a freelance lecturer and writer specialising in children's writing, art and Personal, Social and Moral Education. He has been described as 'the nearest thing I've seen to the Pied Piper'. Previously a headteacher in primary schools for 16 years, he has published books of poetry for both children and adults.

Read my mind

Young children, poetry and learning

Fred Sedgwick

London and New York

First published 1997
by Routledge
11 New Fetter Lane, London EC4P 4EE

Simultaneously published in the USA and Canada
by Routledge
29 West 35th Street, New York, NY 10001

Typeset in Palatino by M Rules

Printed and bound in Great Britain by
Creative Print & Design (Wales), Ebbw Vale

British Library Cataloguing in Publication Data
A catalogue record for this book is available from the British Library

Library of Congress Cataloguing in Publication Data
Sedgwick, Fred.
    Read my mind: young children, poetry and learning / Fred
Sedgwick
        p. cm.
    Includes bibliographical references and index.
    1. Poetry—Study and teaching (Elementary).   2. Poetry—Study
and teaching (Elementary)—Case studies.   3. Poetry—Authorship—
Study and teaching (Elementary).   4. Reader-response criticism.
5. Learning, Psychology of.   I. Title.
    LB1576.S3434   1997
    372.64—dc20   96-35403
    CIP

ISBN 0-415-14343-8 (pbk)

For, especially, my son Daniel

Contents

Preface

The aim of this book is to help those of us who are interested in children and their learning through poem-writing to reflect on, and thereby improve, our practice.

I'm thinking as I write of parents, student-teachers, teacher-trainers, nursery nurses, and classroom helpers, both paid and unpaid. But if I own up, and say my main audience consists of teachers, I do so in the light of two beliefs. The first is that, in a wise society, everyone would want to be a teacher, and only the best would be chosen, while everyone else would fill the other jobs in society, like politician, OFSTED inspector and adviser. And the second is that all of us are teachers, because all of us share moments with children when their discoveries need our help and support. Throughout this book, when I use the term 'teacher', I mean any adult in a school helping a child to learn.

These two beliefs serve to honour my profession in times when it is routinely denigrated, and to put the writing of poetry in the context of learning. They also place a large responsibility on us all.

In the course of case studies, I offer ways forward in the teaching of that unfashionable thing, poetry. But the emphasis is always on adults, as well as children, as active learners, rather than passive receivers of wisdom, because to treat adults – and children – as mere recipients of other people's wisdom is to insult them. Some of these studies come from work teachers have shared with me on my travels as a writer in schools. Others, the larger part, stem from my own work on those travels.

I aim to place poetry at the centre of our practice in English teaching, where it has been replaced in recent years by mechanistic views of language. Many people in power see language as merely a matter of communication between different individuals, or even worse, as a matter of spelling, grammatical and punctuation correctness. I aim to show that poetry has a crucial function, like art, across the curriculum (see Sedgwick and Sedgwick 1996a) because its way of enforcing reflection has powerful implications for our thinking in all subjects. I also want to repeat something David Holbrook wrote: 'If we know what we are doing when we teach poetry then we shall be secure . . . Teaching poetry is the centre of English' (Holbrook 1961: 63).

The introductory section introduces children first, in the shape of some of their poems; and then it discusses some of what children learn (and some of what adults can learn, if they allow it) by writing poetry. I suggest that, in the context of children's learning, the distinction between poetry and science is, to a large extent, an unhelpful one. Both are acts of attention intent on discovery. In the introduction, I also discuss various definitions of poetry, or ways of seeing it.

Part I is made up of case studies of children learning about themselves through writing; first they write about their bodies (chapter 2), and then about their memories, emotions, biographies and personalities (chapter 3). The brief interlude is concerned with two central issues, cliché and drafting, both discussed with examples. Part II is concerned with learning about the outer world: in chapter 5, children use various techniques to get closer to things, and chapter 6 is concerned with writing about nature. There is a note on writing about the human-made environment. Part III suggests that children, critically, learn about their relationship with the world when they write. Chapter 8 discusses death and other obsessions, chapter 9 is about fantasy of various kinds. Chapter 10 contains examples of children writing poetry within the context of the humanities, especially History and Religious Education. Chapter 11 is about writing about love.

In chapter 12 in Part IV, I discuss children responding to poems, showing with examples how children can have creative relationships with poems that are usually considered difficult. The book ends with appendices containing a list of the techniques for getting children writing that I have used in the making of this book, and various select and critical lists of books that support my ideas and entertain children and teachers.

When I look at examples of early, emerging writing by children under the age of five, I am always struck by the resemblance of these documents to tiny lyric poems. I freely acknowledge that some of this resemblance is fortuitous. But it still suggests to me that the word 'story', which is traditionally the genre word most associated with children's writing in schools, is less appropriate than 'poem'. Trailing their clouds of glory, most children are closer to poetry by a long way than most adults are. And I am certain that adults could learn much from children by respecting them more, and listening to them, and reading what they write with a more careful attention than is common.

Acknowledgements

Most books are, in a sense, collaborations. All books about education necessarily are, because they are about the relations (more complex than usually allowed) between the teacher and the learner, the taught and the learnt. I am happy to acknowledge the help of teachers whose work has influenced me in the writing of this book. I am also happy to acknowledge the influence of over a hundred children. They are too numerous, I'm sorry to say, to mention. I hope they'll accept my thanks and my dedication in poor return for their work.

Mary Jane Drummond has given me shining advice, and I would like to thank her, not only for her help with this book, but for her inspiration over a decade of friendship, intermittent conversation and correspondence about young children, teachers and learning.

THE TEACHERS

Dawn Sedgwick, especially, for her work with nursery and reception children; Jane Hodgman; Andrea Durrant; Henry Burns Eliot; Simon Knott; Jacquie Knott; John Lynch; Duncan Allan; Alan Williams; Duncan Bathgate; Gordon Askew.

THE SCHOOLS

Suffolk

Downing Primary, Ipswich
Cliff Lane Primary, Ipswich
Clare Middle
St Mary RCVAP, Lowestoft
Tattingstone Primary, Ipswich
Raeburn Infants, Ipswich
Bentley Primary, Ipswich

Norfolk

Feltwell Elementary, RAF Feltwell
Wroughton Middle, Great Yarmouth
Angel Road First, Norwich
Clackclose Primary, Downham Market

Essex

Doggetts CP, Rochford
Woodville Primary, South Woodham Ferrers
St Paul's, Bentley
St John's Primary, Colchester
East Tilbury Infants

Berkshire

Ryvers Combined, Langley, Slough
Marish First, Langley, Slough
The Hawthorns School, Wokingham

Hertfordshire

Cowley CP, Borehamwood
Swing Gate First, Berkhamsted
Parkgate Junior School, Watford
King's Langley Primary

Lancashire

Whalley Primary School

Cambridgeshire

Guilden Morden Primary

Durham

Acre Rigg Junior, Peterloo

I'm sorry if I've missed anyone.

I would also like to acknowledge some other writers. All of them are listed in my bibliography, but volumes by John Cotton, Sandy Brownjohn, Jill Pirrie and Pie Corbett, and Brian Moses have grown particularly scruffy through much use in my poetry teaching kit. This book is a different sort of book, because I am more concerned with what children learn in the *process* of writing than these writers are, and, possibly, less concerned with the final *product*. But I have developed many of their vibrant ideas here, and am grateful.

Fred Sedgwick 1996

A constant possibility of 'Eureka!'
Poetry as a means of learning

The creative writer does the same as the child at play.

(Freud, quoted in Vernon 1970: 127)

Ten-year-old Alice says after a poetry-drafting session, 'I'm glad I wrote that, I know things I didn't know before . . .' She's written about the box in her head (see chapter 3). I ask what she has learned. 'I thought about things in my life I might've forgotten otherwise . . .'

Nine-year-old Bikram writes about his mother, after the lesson described in chapter 11:

You are the plans
of my drawing
you are the alien
of my passion
you are the story
that moves me . . .
You are the fire
inside me

A third child speaks. She is ten:

Dad

When I see a mirror
I see you.
If I smell Java
or burnt toast
I know you're near.
I feel you

if I'm cold
and all alone.

By writing poetry, children learn, not only about things in their lives they might have forgotten, critical as such learning is, but about the central themes of human existence. Indeed, poetry enables the learner/writer (I am going to argue that they are one and the same) to approach answers to the world, the universe and everything. Committed learners/writers learn about themselves, the world around them (in the examples above, their parents), their relationship with the world, and their language. However dark the environment is, poetry is a continual possibility of light.

These are large, simple claims, and the rest of this book is an attempt, with examples, to justify them. Because poetry exists on the frontier between the known world and the world of the imagination, it reaches out to both. By teaching children to write poetry, we can intensify all their learning – both learning that happens within the confines of the National Curriculum, and learning that happens freed from those confines. We can endow such learning with more sensitivity and strength than we may have thought available to us. Poetry isn't merely another segment in that system of tests and, later, exams. Among all that spelling, grammar and (if we're old enough to remember) parsing, poetry is something more than something teachers teach when the real work has been done. Way beyond all that fiddle, poetry provides muscle for science, history, geography, art, technology, religious education and (above all) those activities usually grouped under the heading of Personal, Social and Moral Education.

We may be surprised in our culture to see poetry linked so closely with, say, science. But this dislocation between the study and the laboratory is not there in some other countries. The Czech poet Miroslav Holub is also an immunologist, and he mixes the languages of science and poetry in an instructive and exhilarating way in an interview in the *Poetry Review* (vol 75: 3). 'In science', he says, 'we think in metaphors. When writing poems, I do an experiment all the time with a possible "yes" and "no" answer.' The western European habit, which places a great gulf between areas of learning – art, science, history, geography – is a sentimental delusion fostered by philistines on both sides who want to keep their hands clean of what they don't understand. For scientists, it may be all the messy emotion that is unavoidable when we try to write about the birth of a son or daughter, or the death of parents; for the artist, s/he may want to avoid exploring the very mechanics of our natural and artificial world. In writing, we as teachers should aim to bring the precision of poetry – that unrelenting, largely conscious search for the right word, and the largely unconscious search for the appropriate sounds, in terms of rhyme, rhythm, assonance and alliteration – to the emotion, the excitement, of science.

Also, as Herbert Spencer says (1929: 41), '. . . science is itself poetic . . . sci-ence opens up realms of poetry where to the unscientific all is a blank'. To understand this, we need only reflect for a moment on scientific images that new technology has shown us: micro-images of the smallest things, images from the inside of the human body, and images from distant space. We might also reflect on how slow-motion film of animals moving opens up the possibility of poetry, and how purposeful, painstaking examination of phenomena, chemical, biological and physical, resembles similar obser-vation that poets use. As the poet George Tardios has said (quoted in Pirrie 1987), 'The world is troubled / With a lack of looking'.

With Personal, Social and Moral Education, poetry can open up discus-sion of issues that obsess us all – death is the most serious example – in a way no other subject can. When a child dies, teachers have to help the other children to understand this event. Reading them the story of Jairus' daughter (Mark 5: 21–43) isn't much help, because 'straightway the damsel arose, and walked . . . ' What we need is poetry, like Ben Jonson's lines on the death of his first son (1975: 26):

Rest in soft peace, and, asked, say here doth lie
Ben Jonson, his best piece of poetry . . .

POETRY AS A PROCESS OF DISCOVERY

The educational power of poetry, like that of all purposeful individual writing (and, come to that, all purposeful art), stems from the fact that it is a *process* of discovery, not a *record* of it. My late father used to tell me to write something down when I'd learned it, to get a grip on it. One of my history teachers dictated notes, so that we could learn from them later (at least, I suppose that's what he thought). But these are two false parts of the same false model. We don't use writing pre-eminently to learn better what we already know, or as a checklist for what we must learn later. On the contrary, many writers have noted how they do not know what they mean for sure until they see what they are writing. They discover their meanings, beliefs and convictions from the words that appear under their hands, or on the screen, instead of (as my father and my history master believed) writing down known meanings, beliefs and convictions.

In other words, they change as they write. They change themselves and the way they think. They change their views of the world, and of the way their imaginations operate on that world. Helen McNeill says of the American poet, Emily Dickinson, that she 'uses her art to break open received certitudes. She is a heuristic poet, a poet of investigation and knowledge . . . Her poetry experiences and argues and questions . . .' (1986: 9). 'Heuristic' is related to 'Eureka!' and comes from the Greek verb 'to find'. The theme of this book is that poetry is a way of finding out, or exploring and learning; it provides a constant possibility of 'Eureka!' throughout our lives. Frank Smith (1982: 1) says in his book on writing: 'the act of writing can tell the author things that were not known (or known to be known) before the writing began . . .' This book is about the attention to life that writing entails, and its rewards.

Simone Weil says, beautifully, about acts of attention that 'one day a light that is in exact proportion to [that attention] will flood the soul'. She is talking here (Panichas 1977: 46) of school exercises. It is certainly no less true of attention paid to trying to understand, say, a scientific experiment, or a Shakespeare play, or a father–son relationship. It is an insight that should invigorate any of us who have ever sat over anything struggling to even begin to understand it: relationship, experiment, historical event, poem. It is effectively the perfect model for any student. Because, not only do we learn about ourselves, and our relationships, emotions, and thoughts when we write, but also about the world, or whatever part of it we are examining at the time. Each effort of study has power in itself.

All this learning is the central element when we teach children to write poetry. It depends crucially on questions about that moment after a child has offered us a draft of a poem. They're all, essentially, the same question: How do we deal with that moment? How do we make sure it is educational? that it is concerned with increasing, or enriching the child's learning, rather than constraining it? Where does our comment stand on a continuum from, at one end, 'Now get on with your maths/science/art' and, at the other, the initiation of a critical, helpful, loving discussion of the draft? How has Avainte, for example, made the extraordinary leap of the imagination that connects two hitherto unconnected ideas, and how should we help her develop her poem?: 'You are/the beautiful mountains/ of Colorado' (see p 152) Her poem is an example of a fresh writer to whom the possibility of divorce between poetry and geography has simply not occurred.

And there is another question: what evidence of learning can we find in children's poems? – about themselves, relationships and language? And I don't only mean learning about what is going on now, but about learning they have already accomplished, about learning that has already taken root. It is commonplace to say that as teachers we don't work with blank slates, with empty bowls in children's minds. But we often behave as if that is exactly what we do believe. What can we, as teachers, learn from this work – interpreting the child's learning past and present and, once again, those relationships?

Finally, can we speculate on where inside the child's consciousness his or her imagination is reaching with the poem? This is obviously more problematic than what we can see of intellectual activity about the known world. It is a very difficult thing to do. But when Coleridge, having owned up to how much he admires Sir Isaac Newton, continues, 'I believe the

Souls of 500 Sir Isaac Newtons would go to the making up of a Shakespeare or a Milton' (Holmes 1989: 302) he isn't denigrating science, I believe, but a mechanistic way of thinking that devalues the invisible behaviour of thought, feeling and what the imagination, with its Janus way of looking in two directions at once, can achieve.

MECHANISTIC THINKING

Now, this mechanistic thinking is prominent in our schools in two domineering modes. The first is behaviourist psychology. Children are routinely removed from their normal classroom setting for assessments based entirely on normative measures. And the influence of this kind of psychology infects the language of teachers as they talk about children and learning. Every time, for example, someone talks about deficiencies in a child's skills, that teacher is using language that comes from behaviourism, and that thereby restricts our view of the child. It makes us think of the child as a bundle of skills gained or not gained, rather than as a complete human being.

The second mode is related to this psychological view. It is composed of the attainment targets of the National Curriculum. The very names – *targets*, related to, if not synonymous with *objectives* – belie the fact that these systems constitute a value system as much as if the elements in it had been called 'subjectives'. In effect, any checklist of objectives is derived from a value–position, though this is rarely stated. Indeed, an attempt at any objective view of things is a daft enterprise, because any looker, anyone trying hard to see what s/he is supposed, or expected, to see, is bound to make something new, however small, out of what s/he sees. The activity of looking is, in other words, a creative act. That is to say, it is an act of deep subjectivity leavened with technique that might make it publishable (that is, public). The making of things out of looking may be next to nothing at all. But, as it may be science, or history, or geography, it may also be a poem.

Both of these systems – behaviouristic psychology and an objectives model of curriculum – are only concerned with the external, the observable, the measurable, the 'skills'. Their grim influence can be seen in this document, which a friend found in a secondary school:

ENGLISH DEPARTMENT THIRD YEAR . . . STUDY OF POETRY

NAME:

has shown the ability to:

1 Compose simple, formal rhymes, e.g. Limericks
2 Recognise figurative language . . .
3 Explain figurative language . . .
4 Compose . . . effective similes and metaphors

Notice how all these objectives are observable and relatively simple ones (six to eight, which I haven't quoted, are similar) until we get to numbers nine and ten, which are simply impossible and absurd. This is just the kind of tangle that writers of objectives will always get into when they approach the big issues: understanding poetry, and the big guns of the poet's armoury, love and pain and death. Such things cannot be measured in terms of objectives of any kind, and when the attempt is made, we leap from the cold wastes of Pluto to the danger of the sun: 'Identify poetic techniques . . . Share the feelings or mood of a poet . . .'

This is in contrast with Eliot's 'auditory imagination', where the observable was only the starting point, the first part of an unobservable process. He would, as Peter Ackroyd has said (1984: 265), construct a 'working model', and then leave his mind to one side. All poetry is to a greater or lesser extent the product of the hidden. Elijah couldn't hear the Lord's voice in the hurricane, the fire or the earthquake. He had to wait for the silence, for the still, small voice (I Kings 19: 11–13).

These are the issues that I am concerned with in this book, and all teachers will accept that they are important issues. Certainly, they may not concern us at those myriad times of the day when the administrative wasps of dinner money, testing and the less elevated parts of the National Curriculum are buzzing irritatingly and (even) dangerously over our heads. But reflection at a more relaxed time will teach us that language's power as a learning tool is paramount over all other tools.

REDEEMING TIME AND ASKING QUESTIONS

We are, of course, nowhere without language. It is what makes us human beings. W H Auden says that time actually worships language, forgiving people who live by it (see 'In Memory of W B Yeats', original version: in Wright 1965: 24–5. The official version in Auden's *Collected Poems* (1976) omits the relevant stanzas). Part of me knows that this is over-stated, and another part knows he is right; because to make our language as sure and adventurous as we can is to underscore and strengthen our humanity. The power of poetry stems from the fact that a poem is like a holiday which, while it is a date in the calendar, is also a break in the sequence of days. A poem can only take place in time, of course, like everything else. But because it uses the elements of time, like rhythm and pauses, it gives us a means to reflect on time. Of course, the effective writer can rearrange past time, as all successful dictators know, making the undesired subversive an 'unperson' by writing him or her out of the books.

Reading an early draft of this introduction, I noticed how often I used words concerned with time: 'moment', 'time' itself and now 'date', 'days' and 'calendar'. The power of poetry extends both ways in time. It can influence our future thinking and feeling, and it can, with a tiny phrase, bring someone into our head who died years ago, much as 'Capstan-stained', 'toadmoled' and 'Cwm Rhondda' in a so-far failed poem of mine summon my father to my head and heart.

There is, as Frank Smith says (1982: 11), 'a profound political issue here'. Not only can the liar change the past, but also, 'writing is revolutionary in that it can conspire to change the order . . .' In other words, it can change the future. That is why politicians, with their passion for power and keeping it, emphasise reading over writing. In a print-oriented world, we need to be able to read in order to follow orders. Gathering books some years ago about the teaching of poetry, I was struck by the fact that all the books I could find published before 1960 were not about the writing of poetry, but the reading of it (see chapter 12 for more on this). The 1960s may have foisted much kaftan-clad rubbish on us, but at least they allowed some of us to understand that poetry lends all of us a voice, if we are attentive to its demands, and the demands of what we are writing about.

Questions

Questions work for all learning better than statements. I suppose that if I were to be asked to draw a line through a list of all the teachers known, dividing those I've admired from those I haven't, it would separate those who asked real questions, and those who didn't. Teachers at one extreme only make statements. Others ask questions that aren't really questions at all, but disciplinary measures or administrative necessities: 'What do you mean by standing there like that?' This is a question that cannot have an answer. Another type of question teachers often use is the question that can have only one answer: 'What are the boats the Vikings came in called?' I have written elsewhere (1994b) that:

> the very few questions to which the teacher doesn't, necessarily, know the answer . . . are often the most productive, the most educational questions: 'What do you mean by that sentence there?' . . . 'How do you think that is working?' . . . 'Why do you believe that?' . . . 'When is that likely to happen?'

This emphasis on reflection and questions, and the link between the two, means that this book is not a series of tips for teachers. There are already many such books available, and the best of them are listed at the end. This book treats both children and teachers as active learners; and, as far as teachers are concerned, being an active learner means taking on ideas and changing; making theories developed out of other people's practice appropriate to ourselves and our children, not merely following instructions from a poetry recipe book. Teachers want to know about theories generated by other teachers' practice, and how those theories affect their classrooms; and, indeed, how those classrooms affect those theories. I use a version of a model developed by Lawrence Stenhouse in *An Introduction to Curriculum Design and Development* (1976). I think that teachers will be defeated by the political pressure generated through (among other things) administrative labour unless they meet frequently to talk to each other about education: about teaching and learning. As this applies to teaching poetry, it means researching each other's work: sharing what the children and we as teachers have written, and, if at all possible, watching each other teach.

Poetry is a medium for teaching many things in the National Curriculum. And, although, as I've said, this is not a book of 'tips', it is full of case studies of teachers teaching and children writing that offer practical advice on how to achieve the National Curriculum's aims. My anxieties about the National Curriculum stem from the fact that it is prescriptive, while poetry is permissive. The National Curriculum power-dresses in a suit and *trains* us, while poetry wears what it fancies (or, more likely, can afford) each morning and attempts to educate us, to take that questioning look at the world and into the imagination, into the past and the future, into the physically unknowable.

POWER OVER LANGUAGE

Admittedly the National Curriculum has some sound things in it. It was, after all, written by what Mark Antony would call 'honourable men':

> Pupils should be given opportunities to write in response to a variety of stimuli, including . . . poems . . . pupils should be taught . . . to describe the movement of familiar things, e.g. cars getting faster, slowing down, changing direction . . . pupils observe a range of animals and plants . . . pupils describe the changes in light . . .
>
> (*National Curriculum* 1995)

Power over language, which the writing of poetry, above all things, gives us, also gives us power over our environment, human and physical, and thereby helps in our relationships with it. We can see the possibilities for this in these quotations from the National Curriculum. But language gives us power in a wider sense. Here are some examples.

First, a teacher is talking on a course:

> About fifteen years ago, we decided we needed more security locks on the doors at home, and a local firm agreed to fit Chubb locks on the doors for fifty pounds. The job was done and we went to Cornwall on

holiday. When we returned, we found a bill waiting for us – for ninety-four pounds!

After a moment's discomfiture I wrote a letter complaining. It was a subtle letter, I now realise; a touch of sarcasm; a suggestion that I knew how the business world worked (which I don't). It was done on my old electric typewriter, with our address at the top, and theirs underneath; and it gave (most important I now think) room for the man receiving my complaint to give way without losing face.

And, of course, he did give way. But if I hadn't had that gift for language, that subtlety, that power, I'd've given in probably, and coughed up.

Other more important examples are the books, poems, plays, articles and journals written in totalitarian countries that have helped provoke huge changes in those countries. Look, for example, at the work of poets like Anna Akhmatova and Irina Ratushinskaya in Russia, and the novelist Breyten Breytenbach in South Africa.

Smaller examples (though the most important ones for us as teachers) are those poems very young children write or dictate to help them come to terms with elements in their lives that distress them:

> I was angry.
> I smacked Paul's hair.
> I was angry.
> I did not want to go to bed early.
> I was angry.
> I drew on the bedroom walls
> and I threw my toys at the wall.
>
> ....
> **Judith, 6**

I argue that the best way of teaching language and thereby helping children to gain power over their world is to teach poetry. This is true, first, because it strengthens the will to avoid cliché. In the Interlude after chapter 3 I discuss cliché at some length, because I am sure that few other concepts can be as important in the task of teaching children to write well. One indispensable condition of poetry, especially, is originality. Indeed, it is probably impossible to conceive of a poem that isn't composed, largely, of sentences that have never been written, or indeed spoken, in the history of the world before. That is why most new poetry is demanding and difficult, even obscure: it won't, as a rule, allow us to fall back on known versions of ways of expressing our thinking and feeling. Second, poetry strengthens our sense of rhythm. It makes it more difficult to write a bureaucratic sentence like this one, just found in an introduction to an article in a book about primary education:

> the author examines how traditional stories help children to 'scale time' as well as offering teachers some valuable evidence about how young writers use stories firmly embedded in their culture to articulate their own contemporary cultural experience – in this case expressed in gendered identification.

(Bearne 1995)

Third, it has an appeal to the senses that other writing has, usually, only to a lesser extent. This wonderful sonnet, Shakespeare's 130th, demonstrates all three of these points:

> My mistress' eyes are nothing like the sun,
> Coral is far more red, than her lips red,
> If snow be white, why then her breasts are dun:
> If hair be wires, black wires grown on her head:
> I have seen roses damasked, red and white,
> But no such roses see I in her cheeks,
> And in some perfumes there is more delight,
> Than in the breath that from my mistress reeks.
> I love to hear her speak, yet well I know,
> That music hath a far more pleasing sound:
> I grant I never saw a goddess go,
> My mistress when she walks treads on the ground.
>   And yet by heaven I think my love as rare,
>   As any she belied with false compare.

(Sonnets: 130)

The poem is, first, an explicit and devastating attack on cliché. Imagine the opposite of that beginning: My mistress' eyes are like the sun, her lips are red as coral, her breasts are white as snow . . . Indeed, Shakespeare is here turning a whole culture of love poetry on its head, and he attacks a stereotypical notion of the beautiful loved woman as a blonde, rosy-cheeked, quietly-spoken, sweet-smelling possession. In its rejection of that stereotype, this poem stands up for that indispensable condition of all poems: it must be new.

The rhythm convinces us of the authenticity of the poet's experiences in, for example, the words 'walks treads on the ground', where the line, obedient to the poet's will and his mistress's walk, trudges (note the contrast with the way a goddess simply 'goes'); and the poem has that sharp appeal to all the senses: the smell of the woman that 'reeks' from her, her voice which the poet loves to hear, while acknowledging that 'music hath a far more pleasing sound'. (Incidentally, the pejorative sense of the word 'reek', 'stinks', was unknown to Shakespeare, Martin Seymour-Smith tells us in his edition of the *Sonnets*, 1963.) The use of concrete nouns ('coral', 'wires', 'roses') and the lack of abstract ones also contribute to the poem's immediacy. Reading poems like this enriches our language; writing under the influence of such poems makes us more vigorous writers and speakers.

Finally, we can usefully, if somewhat insolently, I suppose, speculate on Shakespeare's learning as he wrote these lines; about this woman, and his perception of her; and about all men's previous perceptions of women.

However, poetry has, I know, a bad reputation. It starts, as the Bullock Report commented, 'at a disadvantage . . . it is either numinous . . . or an object of comic derision'(1975: paragraphs 9.22–9.23). Elizabeth Bennet in *Pride and Prejudice* talks about 'the efficacy of poetry in driving away love'. The Victorian Evangelical Christian Hannah More exclaimed, when someone mentioned the subject: 'Poetry! oh! as to poetry, I forswore that, and I think everybody else should forswear it, together with pink ribbons' (quoted in Lindop 1981:182). The definition of poetry implicit in these remarks suggests that it is something ineffectually decorative and flippant; that it might be useful for the young and unserious, but we who know more are above it. A widespread perception of poetry as a sloppy sentimental thing is captured perfectly by James Joyce in the words of his character, Gerty MacDowell, in *Ulysses*: '. . . she felt that she too could write poetry if she could only express herself like that poem that appealed to her so deeply that she had copied it out of the newspaper she found one evening round the potherbs. Art thou real, my ideal? . . .' Poetry is not this gluey escape from the reality of the potherbs and the bits and pieces of our everyday life. To make it that is to disempower it. It is altogether different. It is the opposite of an escape. Not a prison, but an unremitting, loving examination of the place where we are, both in the world and in the imagination, both in time and in space.

In my reading about poetry (and the other arts) the image of the prison has occurred time and time again. We must put art in prison before we can set it free. Unstructured verse constrains and makes things uniform. It is essentially totalitarian, because it insists on its own rhetoric and the shape that rhetoric takes (or, more often, doesn't take). It is in control. Learning about techniques, on the other hand, sets the writer free, because in the search for rhymes, alliterations and assonances, the mind searches systematically for options.

Furthermore, it is a terrible fact, an almost uncontemplatable one, that poets in prisons, literally, often get closer to the essence of poetry than those of us who live in near-democracies. While in harmonious societies there will always be good and sometimes great poems about love, death, moss, the sound of a guitar, the burning flame produced by lead compounds, fear and children – not to mention ones about how stupid and dull politicians are – in societies where poets and others are imprisoned for their beliefs and works, the pressure will always be on for poets to address the extremes of human behaviour, the terrors and the sacrifices. And the politicians will be, not only stupid and dull, but wicked and dangerous as well. Audiences understand, through their oppression, the necessity of poetry. Witness Anna Akhmatova's terrible story (told in Akhmatova 1976: 23). As she queued outside Stalin's prisons with other women waiting to see their husbands, lovers and sons, one woman whispered to her, 'Can you describe this?' In conditions like this, poetry achieves its true status of unacknowledged legislator. In our society, it is seen by most people (to judge from the sales of books) as something irretrievably minor. Most books about primary education don't bother even mentioning it.

DEFINING POETRY

Now there are many more or less serious definitions of poetry. Poetry is:

> what makes my toenails twinkle . . . lines without end . . . a comforting piece of fiction set to lascivious music . . . a mere drug . . . the Honey of all Flower, Marrow of Art . . . sissy stuff that rhymes . . . the best words in the best order . . . a pheasant disappearing in the brush . . . the newspaper of the world that is to come . . . life distilled . . . the ashes of a burnt-out passion

These come, in turn, from Dylan Thomas, R Williams Parry, H L Mencken, George Farquhar, Thomas Nashe, Nigel Molesworth (in *Down with Skool!*, by Willans and Searle 1958), S T Coleridge, Wallace Stevens, Louis Aragon, Gwendolyn Brooks and Oliver Wendell Holmes. I put this list together because I think its quirkiness suggests that there are more ways of looking at poetry than are dreamed of in our philosophy. Thanks for it to Meic Stephens and his *Dictionary of Literary Quotations* (Stephens 1990). Not many women there, says my friend. And she is right. This fact reflects the dominance of men in their access to the means of publication. But, in any case, those who crave definitions might bear in mind the advice of Dunn *et al.* (1987) who say that teachers 'teach best when they don't accept the unspoken definition of poetry . . . and instead forge a definition that has a particular meaning for them'. Indeed, the act of defining poetry is something of a contradiction in terms, because definitions are about generalising, and poetry is about the particular.

Defining things is all too often a puritanical legalism that enables people to say later, 'That isn't poetry . . .' (or art or music or whatever) 'because it doesn't conform to what we agreed . . .' And, as Geoffrey Grigson puts it in his book about poetry, *The Private Art* (1982), 'Why are we always asking for definitions of poetry? "No, no! The adventures first," said the Gryphon in an impatient tone: "explanations take such a dreadful time".' Indeed, defining things always pulls us in a conservative direction, as if we have to measure up to statements about the art made before we were born. Perhaps children should be constructing definitions for themselves, in conversation with each other and their teachers. John Ruskin says that '. . . the imagination is always right. It evidently cannot err . . . the composing [or defining] legalism does nothing else than err' (quoted in Hourd 1949: 82).

There are various kinds of definitions of poetry, and all of them represent a kind of conforming legalism. There is the hierarchical kind, used by certain poets when talking about education. For example, Vernon Scannell has written that

> young children do not write poems, and never have done . . . A poem is the exploration and shaping of an experience . . . And to make a poem, a real poem, demands intelligence, imagination, passion, understanding, experience . . . and a knowledge of the craft . . .
>
> (Scannell 1977: 74ff)

This is really both a blustering defence of a vested interest and a stunningly disrespectful comment on children. Children do have intelligence, imagination, passion, understanding and experience. Children can invent a world and its inhabitants, and this is an activity far beyond most adults. Has Scannell, I wonder, never seen the passion in a child's face as s/he meets her baby sister/brother for the first time, or indignantly tells the story of an injustice? All children have understanding, too, though arguably less than us.

Of course children have had experiences just as adults have – only fewer of them. Mole also is dismissive that 'the child is a natural poet [. . . this is] . . . a sentimental fallacy . . .' (in Bagnall 1973: 189). But Causley looks at children's poems from another, potentially more creative perspective:

> . . . the child possesses by nature that valuable quality all adult artists seek to retain or regain: the ability of being able to view the world . . . as if for the first time . . . unblurred by time and experience and tact and expediency . . .
>
> (Rogers 1979)

Freud (in Vernon 1970) points out that children at play behave like creative writers, in the way in which they rearrange the objects in their worlds to make that world more pleasing to them.

I think both points of view are true. Children do need teaching in the craft; and they are also real poets. And this is my way of finding a way through this discrepancy. Learning by heart and experimenting with form are ways of setting children free. If you have to search for words – because they rhyme, or have the right syllabic structure, or have what appears to be (at the time of drafting) an appropriate sound – then you are choosing and rejecting, considering and reflecting. You are making discoveries. And in this search, far from being imprisoned, you are getting closer and closer every minute to the heart of your being, to your nerves. You are paying attention to what the language can help you find out about being you, and also to what you can find out about the language.

To be told, on the other hand, 'Write a poem about your feelings' you are as free as a person in the middle of a desert. That person is free to go any-where within his or her reach – but that is not very far, and the journey is not very pleasant. And, of course, the freedom is illusory.

Then there is the cultural definition: how poetry is seen by most people, and I suspect that Gerty MacDowell in *Ulysses* sums that up. Poetry is a sentimental thing that expresses the innermost romantic longings of men and women. I once sifted the entries for a national children's poetry com-petition on the subject of water, and learned there that poetry is defined by most people with notions that revolve around romantic images, often pla-giarised ones. Coleridge's line 'Water water everywhere' figured at least two hundred times in my batch of 40,000 poems, and so did Masefield's 'I must down to the seas again', usually misquoted, probably because of Finzi's song, as 'I must go down to the seas again'. Writers often used archaic diction ('so endeth my song') as though poetry was caught in a pre-industrial time warp (Sedgwick 1988: 69).

This definition of poetry is part of the 'fag-end' of the romantic move-ment, and is prominent in spite of Wordsworth's remark at the beginning of *Lyrical Ballads* that a poet should be a 'man speaking to men'. When I read poems by adults who use phrases like 'sojourn in that fair academic town' (real example) when they mean 'lived in Cambridge' I know that the dominant cultural definition of poetry is a sentimental harking back to better times that never existed. And what children produce is often a well-meaning attempt at what they think their teacher, as a representative of all that's powerful, thinks is a poem.

There is, in this definition of poetry, a notion that technique will some-how falsify the true feeling with which poetry is essentially concerned; that all we need is sincerity and then everything else will follow. I think that there is an analogy here with the Christian theology of faith and works. Orthodox belief teaches believers that all they need is their faith. But 'faith without works is dead', writes St James (James 2: 17). Thus, while sincerity is enough in a human way, it is like faith on its own. Sincerity, we might say, without technique, is dead. Another, more homely, analogy might be with aspects of family life. We believe strongest in the kind of love that expresses itself in acts. Certainly the love that exists, and yet sits in the chair while the meal is prepared, may be, indeed, love. But it is dead compared with the love that helps in the preparation.

Technique is central. It is more than craft, which could be simply copying another writer's style. It involves a mysterious mixture of emotion, or feeling, and the shape in which that feeling is to be expressed. I am sure that, as we struggle technically with a poem (with metaphor, for example, or rhythm, or rhyme, or alliteration, all of which are discussed later in this book), the emotion is doing its work on us. Inspiration isn't separable from perspiration, then, as in the old adage, but comes *through* the perspiration.

To write a pastiche of a poet one admires is a useful step in the learning of the craft. You can pick up tricks of metre and rhyme, even metaphor and simile. Technique goes much further, involving as it does the articulation of one's own voice, and the making of that voice public.

Children defining poetry

Thinking it would be useful to have a definition of poetry that came from children, I gave a class of seven- and eight-year-olds a questionnaire which asked: What is a poem? What must all poems have? What do you like about poetry? And hate about it? This could have been more sensitively written, of course, but the children responded with vigour. A poem is (all spelling corrected):

> a quick piece of writing . . . it's kind of a rhyme, it's a big riddle . . . it rhymes . . . like a short story but it rhymes . . . a piece of writing that rhymes . . . a rhyming story . . . rhyming . . . a rhyme . . . a piece of writing that rhymes . . . it rhymes . . .

Some of the children didn't think poems had to rhyme – but the word 'rhyme' still figured largely in their sentences. It was always an issue:

> It is something that sometimes don't rhyme . . . it is something that rhymes but sometimes don't and it is like a short story . . . it is a story that sometimes rhymes . . .

This little survey was done in a class where the teacher is a passionate reader of poetry, and yet still rhyme figured as the indispensable condition of poetry. I know that I have said that the search for rhyme is a liberating experience, but it is odd that rhyme is the only condition of poetry that the children thought necessary. This probably comes from nursery rhymes and, possibly, popular music. But it must be said, also, that most writers for children do use rhyme. But even more constricting conditions were to follow: What must all poems have?

> . . . a full stop . . . capital letters and full stops . . . a title . . . a full stop . . . a title . . . capital letters and full stops . . . rhymes . . . words that rhyme . . . a story in it . . . full stops and the right spellings . . .

There is a gulf between a notion of poetry that is essentially correct spelling and punctuation, and one that sees it as a process of learning; as a line between the writer and the rest of the world, tingling electrically with possibilities. I am not saying here that poems shouldn't be correct in grammatical and punctuation terms; merely that such terms aren't the first things a poet is thinking of as s/he writes. If we are to make the child–writer's experience as close as possible to the adult–poet's experience, we would do well to help them see their exercise books as notebooks. We would do well not to insist on dates at the top and neat margins and underlinings.

The answers to questions about liking poetry nearly always involved humour. The keyword in the responses was 'funny'. This was repeated over 20 times. And several children wrote about how they hated 'sad' poems, though they also hated poems that were

> . . . a bit long . . . [that had] long words . . . hard words what I can't read . . . too long words . . .

Humour and poetry do have much in common, because both are concerned with the yoking together of the previously separated. A joke makes us laugh, if it does at all, by surprising us with a link. A mother sits with a baby on her knee. The baby gurgles at her with a big, charming smile, eyes wide with love and need. And the mother says, 'I do wish you'd stop trying to talk until you can do it properly'. This yokes together the charm of a baby and a parent's stern sentence that would only be appropriate to a very different setting. As a joke, it serves another purpose: of course, no sane parent would say anything like that to a child. But as adults, we do sometimes behave in that way about writing: You can't write a poem until you've got all your letters formed properly.

It was encouraging to me that the idea of the riddle came up in the children's answers, because riddles have a similar relationship to poetry as jokes. They also draw together the previously unattached. I demonstrate the power of the riddle in poetry in chapter 5.

Eight children, asked the question 'What do you hate about poetry?', responded, with startling and encouraging bluntness: 'Nothing' – a potent compliment, probably, to their teacher.

GETTING THE WORLD RIGHT

My definition of poetry is put best in this line. It's Wallace Stevens again, quoted in Stephens (1990):

> Poetry is a response to the daily necessity of getting the world right.

Using intense language and the traditional techniques of rhyme (sometimes) and rhythm (always) and metaphor and simile, poetry is one of the ways of learning about the world and how it is, and how I can live best in it. For me, poetry is, in Robert Frost's marvellous phrase, a 'temporary stay against confusion'.

But take note: we might get the world right for a moment. We may stay, daily, close to the necessity of attention. But poetry never lets us forget that the potential of confusion is there. That we die. And that we die in a totally unpredictable way. 'I like a look of Agony / Because I know it's true,' writes Emily Dickinson (No. 241 in Thomas H Johnson's edition of *The Complete Poems*, 1970). She is facing away from the temporary stay, and gazes into the chaos. One feels certain, reading this astonishing line, that Dickinson would have agreed with Roland Barthes' remark in his essay on Gide: 'Incoherence seems to me preferable to a distorting order' (Barthes 1982: 3).

Poetry provides a way for us to research the differences and similarities between ourselves and the rest of the world. It provides us with a provisional, shifting verbal object on which we can reflect in order to learn. All that sentimental stuff – 'art thou real my ideal' – isn't poetry. It's something else: a sentimental escape? Poetry, by contrast, I will show, is the teacher that everyone needs, that helps us do those terrible and beautiful experiments with yes and no answers, that helps us to look into the chaos with the occasional reassuring glance at the sustaining order.

> I'm glad I wrote that, I know things I didn't know before . . . I thought about things in my life I might've forgotten otherwise . . .

Alice, and your friends: be witnesses with your poems to these truths.

Part I

Part I

Chapter 1

Introduction

Most precious words

When I was angry
I screamed and I
stamped my feet
and I scribbled
on the walls
I was quiet for
a long time.
I said sorry
that was all
right then
it was all
back to
together
again
the
end

....
Jenny, 5

In this part I will look at some poems in which there is evidence of children learning about themselves. There is such learning in almost all children's writing, of course, but I am concerned here with a particular kind, where the teaching, the learning and the writing are all helping us to look inwards; first to the body, and second to the personality. The theoretical structure that holds much of this part together is, to use religious language, prayer, or, to use more neutral language, meditation. Each of us carries inside him or herself the face of God, a unique icon designed in negotiation with – or opposition to – that God over years of thought and experience. But for those who believe in God without being aware of it, I will take some of the metaphysical heat out, and say I am concerned here with reflection and attention ('I was quiet for/a long time').

I don't apologise for the religious language I use here and elsewhere in this book. Following art is, in some ways, little different from following religion. Both require intense preoccupation. Both need these intense silences, with eyes either closed, or open and focused on the image, or idea, to the point where it might hurt. Both are concerned with the big themes that have concerned all humanity from the beginning: love and death, of course, but also (a manifestation of love) how we build our relationships with the world we live in. Both take the apparently random nature of the millions of facts we know (or think we know) about the world, and stare them out, insisting on structure, or meaning, or, at least, significance. And both religion and art use symbols as a central part of their structure, and images of religion have seeped inexorably into our language and our poetry.

Crucially, both religion and art (perhaps this sums up the essence of all their common elements) fight against a mechanistic, materialistic view of humankind; a view that devalues reflection, and the use of time to help us come to terms with our human situation. Turning to our main concern, the education of children, I note that thought, or deliberation, or concentration, or reflection are all discouraged by certain classroom habits. For example, the moment a hand is shot up in response to a teacher's 'Now, who can tell me . . .', the brain, the heart and the spirit are disengaged, and the child's objective is to gain attention, affection, respect, who knows what?, but not understanding. S/He has become, for the moment, a cog in a machine, a mere conditioned reaction to a positive reinforcement. Of course, children's thinking is not, in any but the crudest senses, behaviourally observable, and therefore it is devalued in the National Curriculum, which concentrates on the observable.

Another mechanistic element of modern schooling, which both poetry and religion oppose, is a view of children's learning merely in terms of what is prescribed for them. This neglects the richness and unpredictability that children themselves bring to school, and vastly overrates attainment targets. It is encapsulated in the Second National Curriculum (1995) where 'poem' is, typically, reduced to the backs of little lists, and where, in contrast, 'punctuation', 'spelling' and 'handwriting' head dreary paragraphs. Worse, 'layout and presentation' are central features. Presentation matters far more than thought, feeling and content in this document, and we must conclude from it that children's humanity is subservient to their ability to make accurate marks in offices, and to present pleasing letters to employers.

Children must be helped to reflect on themselves. This is not to say that they do not do it all the time. 'I'm very sad', says our three-year-old godson, after he's been stopped from doing something that would endanger his health, if not his life. 'I'm very, very sad.' Later, after spending an hour hurling stones into the estuary, he says, 'I'm tired and I need a cuddle and my bottle and my bed'. But we can provide opportunities for reflection in schools. Look what happens, for example, when we ask children to write down their 'six most precious words'. This is developed from John Cowper Powys (quoted in Dowding 1994), who said that his were 'Key, silver, grass, away, kite and wave. (I hesitate a little between grass and earth. What a beautiful sound EARTH is and so is AIR.)'

The lists below were written by children of eight and nine years old. Following Dowding's example, I asked them to write down in secret their 'six favourite/most precious words'. I didn't want collusion for obvious reasons, and I find secrecy a powerful notion: it hints at the importance of the activity:

> special, Anastasia-kriptic, beautiful, italic, swept, dogs (**Sophie**)

> great, brilliant, frost, pancake, infinity, hippo (**Jenny**)

> beetroot, sunset, red, tickly, elephant, pig (**Stephanie**)

> space, moonlight, animals, stars, shells, sea (**Jacqueline**)

> scrumptious, silly, sausage, fireworks, sunrise, rabbit (**Dawn**)

> flower, rabbit, Christian, help, vegetarian, baby (**Sharon**)

What is going on here? One of Mary Jane Drummond's points (1993) is that, if we are to assess children's learning, we must know them as whole people, and this exercise reveals to us, very quickly, with an alarming suddenness, much about the children's characters in the 'emotional domain'. We cannot, she says:

> without doing violence to our understanding of children as human beings . . . ignore either the emotional turbulence of their lives, or the emotional development that runs alongside the physical, social and cognitive changes that we see taking place in our schools and classrooms.
>
> (Drummond 1993)

Looking back to Dawn's list, we can see evidence of a playful personality (though it is important not to stereotype on this basis, as on any other). In Jenny's, we see the list spin and change direction like a table tennis ball with a wicked slice on it. It teaches us not to take children's outward personalities for granted. Stephanie's list puzzles us, as all glimpses into another person's thinking will, at one time or another.

Dowding, a teacher of six- and seven-year-olds, puts it well:

> The children rose to [the challenge] in an incredibly individual and creative way; their choices, in contrast to those in the Department for Education's tests, were consciously differentiated; each child wanted six words of his or her own, yet they were happy to discuss and compare their choices aloud . . . Each child's choice seemed to spring from deep wells of individuality, from memories, affections, hopes and fears.

In asking children about their favourite words, we acknowledge parts of their (and our) humanity that mechanistic educators ignore. We travel beyond the numbers game we must, by order, play these days, with levels, tests, targets, cost effectiveness and league tables. It is also true that, as the children work on choosing their words, they not only reveal parts of their 'emotional domain'; they also reflect, consciously, half-consciously, or subconsciously, on their own natures. They learn about themselves and their emotional turbulence. Who, having written (to quote two adult examples) 'path, poem, jazz, cadenza, coriander, sunlit' or 'avocado, jasmine, contingent, spikenard, renaissance, therefore', doesn't then pause, frown – and ask, 'What do I mean?'

Robin Skelton says in his book *Poetic Truth* (1978) that almost all words have associations for us. They resonate in the mind and the heart, probably vibrating further in our dreams and (who knows?) after our deaths. Take the list 'special, Anastasia-kriptic, beautiful, italic, swept, dogs'. 'Italic', for example, sends me into handwriting, print and classical history. 'Swept' implies cleanliness and hairstyles, brushes and brooms, putting on a decent show. 'Anastastia-kriptic' is at least something to do with a just-about-remembered pretender to the throne of Russia. These lists demonstrate that no poem (or list of words) has an existence on its own; each such list (and each poem) resonates wildly and creatively in the reader's heart and brain, as well as the writer's.

Eight-year-old James ('not', said his teacher, 'one of our ablest') chose as his favourite words:

crystal, sea, glitter, stars, furry, prickly.

I asked him to use all these words in a sentence. He needed three:

> I went in the sea and I found a crystal. The crystal is starry and prickly at the sides. The shell that it came in was very furry and when I returned the shell in the sea it was like glitter.

He had been writing haikus (those little poems, derived from the Japanese, that only have 17 syllables: five in the first line, seven in the second, and five in the third), and we discussed which words need not be there. He crossed out the second crystal, and I wrote down at his dictation and his counting:

I went in the sea
and I found a crystal. It
is starry, prickly

at the sides. The shell
it came in was a furry and
when I returned it

to the sea, the sea
was like glitter –

'We haven't enough syllables . . .' I began, and he said, 'Let's put the crystal back there!' and the poem ended

– and crystal
reminds me of the sea.

....
James, 8

There is something of importance here to learn – for the teachers and for me. It concerns, first, a reassessment of the child's potential, and of our expectations and what those expectations do to us. Years ago, I watched a headteacher putting ceramic sculptures on a display in a corridor, and he said, they only get broken if you expect them to. An exaggeration, I thought then. Now I think it's a hyperbole, an emphasis on the truth by over-statement. With James's poem, I, who had no expectations, and who therefore, a little blandly, I suppose, expected the best, helped James write some telling words: telling in that they told himself and us something about his personality. But after reading 'crystal, sea, glitter, stars, furry, prickly', are we going, with any confidence, to assess children in mechanistic ways again?

There is also food for thought here for James, who finds that his words, 'crystal, sea, glitter, stars, furry, prickly', can act as roots for a poem that important (to him) adults will recognise. Therefore, his self-esteem is enhanced, and therefore, again, his potential for future learning.

As my deadline for this book approached, I met two boys in a Watford school. Both were nine. One, Aldin, was a refugee from Bosnia. He had told his teacher about fighting for loaves of bread. His six words were 'strong, big, storm, kicked, blood, football'. The other boy, Raheel, was a Muslim. His devotion came across in his words as clearly as the violence of Aldin's past came across in his: 'ALLAH, Mohammed, Gabriel, Akeel, Pakistan, Saudi Arabia'.

KNOW THEN THYSELF

It's easy to find references in English literature (and no doubt in all other literatures) to self-knowledge. 'Know then thyself, presume not God to scan./The proper study of mankind is man' says Pope's couplet (in his 'Essay on Man'), and among Polonius' advice to his son in *Hamlet* there is wisdom (despite the old man's dramatic function as both political busy-body and foil to the prince's cruel wit). We see this especially in his words: 'to thine own self be true/And it must follow as the night the day/Thou canst not then be false to any man'. And we can't be true to ourselves without some self-knowledge. If we don't know ourselves, that 'special, Anastasia-kriptic', how do we know who to be true to?

This part is about self-knowledge and, to be more explicit, about helping children to gain self-knowledge. There are two serious problems here. One was articulated years ago by a novelist who said on television something like: 'Self-knowledge is all very well as long as you are a nice chap'. Self-knowledge may well involve suffering – it certainly does as far as I am concerned, and often I shy away from looking too closely at the myself that seems to make up me. And we should not be sentimental about children knowing themselves, and what, exactly, they know. Many years ago, a child wrote in my company and under a stimulus I'm going to describe later in this part, 'There is no box in my head, and if there was one it would be dark . . . everything in my box is hidden . . .'

The notion that all children are sunny beings is a fallacy constructed largely for commercial purposes. Most of them are for much of the time, but the happiest children have their darkest moments, and life has brought some children little light except that which somehow they can supply for themselves. Marie's mother, her teacher tells me on the way back to the staffroom, died of AIDS. Marie runs alongside me, craving, I suppose, attention, and waves at me from outside the staffroom window as I drink coffee. 'Hi' her mute lips say. And when Jimmie is asked to write about early losses (see chapter 3), he writes, 'Where's the friend/I played with/all day long/when I was five?/Committed suicide in Scotland' (names changed). 'Emotional turbulence' (to quote Drummond 1993 again) doesn't seem quite strong enough, sometimes.

It is inhuman to pretend that all children might stand in for Disney child-heroes and heroines. Those figures are freckled automatons, and they suggest an ideal no child should have to try to live up to: always cheerful and honest, and disobedient only insofar as they are more informed about ethical considerations than their parents. They know, for example, as no human would, that the dolphin Flipper in the Disney film needs his/her love, and will eventually save the island. What is impressive and moving about Marie and Jimmie bears no resemblance to Disney images, but is how they manage to raise their heads time after time above the dirty water in which hours and hours of their lives have been drowned in death and despair and disease. To teach children to write intensively is to enable them to edge away from stereotypes, Disneyesque or otherwise, and to help children to come to terms with their worst experiences, as well as their best ones. We must never suggest that life and art might proceed without pain.

This book is about teaching self-knowledge through poetry. Perhaps that sounds like a contradiction: surely children can only gain knowledge by themselves, and any teacher, however sensitive, will get in the way? If the first problem is that self-knowledge isn't necessarily a relationship with a nice person, the second is this: surely children must, simply, express *themselves* (to go to the roots of that phrase, to 'press themselves out'), to gain self-knowledge, and to help the world gain knowledge of them? Teaching will only get in the way. If we see self-knowledge like that, we ought to bear in mind two things.

The first is that there is much pressure on us all, and, in particular, on our pupils, not to express themselves for their own purposes, but merely to respond, in their lives in general and in their writing in particular, to other people's demands. Advertising is a prime example of how this works. It teaches us, not to focus on ourselves, each other and our human needs, but on our supposed material needs. It pretends to be concerned with us as customers, but really its only concern is with company profits. This duplicity is pointed up in the fact that advertising uses poetic techniques for non-poetic purposes. Two examples are hyperbolic metaphor and punning: 'There's a tiger in my tank . . . All brogue and no blarney' (the latter for a pair of shoes). Advertising debases rhetoric to commercial persuasion. It is commonplace that children are surrounded by print from the moment of their birth, and that from a very early age they have a relationship of one kind or another with that print. It is also true that, in advertising and head-lines, they are surrounded by a kind of poetry that uses, not only rhetoric and hyperbole, but also assonance, alliteration, puns and a strong rhythm, as well as many other poetic devices.

The second reason why the teaching of self-knowledge is so important is that much schooling ushers children in the opposite direction from the one where children might gain more self-knowledge. I've already mentioned the competitive thrust implied in the need to get hands up early to answer questions. There is also the lack of quiet and time to reflect on what they are doing, and their relationship with whatever that is. There is the dragooning into lines and uniforms ('You'd think it was the bloody army' I heard Harold Rosen say in a lecture at Great Offley, in Hertfordshire, 14 June 1996). There are those competitive elements (reading schemes and lists of children showing what arithmetic tables they've learnt, for example) that make a race out of what, by contrast, requires calm reflection.

What a mess it all is: advertising, competition, the lack of time, crass managerial obsessions with cost-effectiveness, levels and all the rest of the manic busy-ness of so-called schooling! In this context, poetry is an adversarial exercise. It refuses its consent. In contrast to advertising, which is concerned solely with selling, poetry has to be true. And this search for the truth requires an integrity that takes time and thought; that, always, sooner or later, subverts the ready-made images, the clichés, the stereotypes, the templates that the powerful in society try to impose. This means, not that poetry is necessarily factually true, but that it must have a scrupulous and mythical wholeness we can trust. Poetry must convince us that the poet isn't saying something merely for effect, as politics (and, of course, advertising) literally is.

'Poetic truth' (Giambattista Vico wrote in 1725)

> is metaphysical truth, and physical truth which is not in conformity with it should be considered false.
>
> (in Hawkes 1977)

This suggests that the facts of imaginative literature are metaphysical truths. We know that Fitzwilliam Darcy and Elizabeth Bennet loved each other in spite of the pride and prejudice of each because Jane Austen has told us so in her chosen medium, the lie of the novel. And, because of that lie, we know a little more than we did about our own feelings, our own pride, our own prejudice. We know about Hamlet's intellectual and moral confusion, and thence a little more about our own. Wordsworth's sneaking the boat out, in Book 1 of the *Prelude* (lines 372–427 in the 1805 text), teaches us about our own childhoods and the minor misdemeanours that seemed like dreadful wickednesses at the time.

We know that this poem (written under the simple stimulus of prepositional phrases: 'behind my face . . . inside my head' etc) is true:

Behind my face
and inside my head
the blood rushes

like people running
to catch a train
in a far-off station
which is beyond the stars.

Through my brain
rattle the days
of the past
and the bad and good.
Over my mind
passes round the work
that has to be done.

Along the silent path
that is secret
there will be red roses
that are prisoned
in my brain.

....
Emma, 10

(from Sedgwick 1989)

But by contrast, we know that the politician is lying when s/he says 'My only interest is the interest of Britain' – because s/he and his or her colleagues have told us so, in their medium, the truth-insisting medium of the television that is so often a lie. We know almost for sure that the politician's main interest is really his or her own well-being, just as we know the advertiser is only concerned with sales and profit, however many 'customer service points' his clients install in stores. We know that both of them are, in Auden's gross and perfect word, 'pound-noteish' (Auden 1976: 527). It is only in our century, which has taken materialism to extremes, that Vico's statement above would provoke much surprise. But, as Mandelstam wrote (1981: 25), 'Is the material thing really the master of the world?' Poetry (and not just Auden's poetry) says, constantly, that when our concerns with money override our concerns with each other, we are in the serious dark. Poetry challenges the money-changers at the door of the temple.

In the context of the teaching of self-knowledge, we need to remember that when children tell about themselves untaught, they merely lay their feelings out for examination. This is part of that definition of poetry I discussed in my introduction, which sees poetry as 'a sentimental thing that expresses our innermost romantic longings'. In this view, the poet is either a self-indulgent person or a brave one. Now this exposure of our feelings may well be an important activity in certain circumstances. The words prayer, meditation, analysis and journal all come to mind here, again. But while each of these may have a contribution to make to writing, whether children's or adults', none of them has had anything *necessarily* to do with either poetry or teaching.

Technique is the medium whereby the expression of those feelings might be made publishable. As teachers, we need to initiate children in various techniques for writing. Technique is that often-forgotten bridge between our feelings and the readable (let alone publishable) expression of them. When children concentrate on technique, their feelings become clearer, both to themselves and their readers. Much as a difficult poem has an effect on us as we concentrate on understanding it, so child–writers expose their meaning through their technical efforts. Work, in both cases, reveals faith.

Here is an example. I had given this eleven-year-old girl a prose version of Gerda Mayer's poem 'Fragment' (Sedgwick 1994a: 3). She had then written:

> My Dad
> raised a flute to the sky
> on a low hill.
>
> The wind of Wales
> puffed some notes
> that were yellow, giant and elf
>
> in the moonlight
> like a red rose.
>
> We are feeble ghosts
> from the ageing years.
>
> A soft beautiful sound.

Whatever is behind this piece was, I suggest, inexpressible without the technique involved in examining, at a significant distance, Mayer's poem: the tone of which, in a crude way, my version had preserved.

But the teacher doesn't merely instruct in technique. Teaching itself is a technique s/he must teach his/her writers. S/He must teach them to teach themselves, and each other. Child–writers have to learn how to quiz their drafts, so that answers will make them better. They will learn more as they learn to edit each other's notes with pointed questions: 'What do you mean by that? What kinds of trees/flowers/cats? What is that word doing there? Can you be more specific about that?'

Blake would have disagreed with this emphasis on teaching:

> I do not believe that Rafael taught Michel Angelo, or that Michel Angelo taught Rafael, anymore than I believe the Rose teaches the Lily how to grow, or the Apple teaches the Pear Tree how to bear fruit.
>
> (quoted in Grigson 1982: 144)

But Blake, though a visionary, was a man of his time, and by 'teach' here he means 'instruct'. I understand something less didactic than that, however. To teach may be to imprison (in a classroom, in a textbook, in a set of handed on ideas), but it is also to set free. To teach is to give 'more than usual order' so that a given poem may disclose 'a more than usual state of emotion' (to use Coleridge's phrases, quoted in Hourd 1949: 174). It is through teaching and technique that the 'opposite and discordant qualities of the mind' become 'balanced and reconciled'. The writer can do without neither the *opposed/discordant* nor the *balanced/reconciled*. It needs the more than usual feeling, and the more than usual order. By implication this requires the vital presence of both. And this presence, of course, is palpably there in Blake, wherever you look.

Chapter 2

'I see me in her eye'
Learning about the body

Here are some lines from children's poems:

> When we pull a fist it's like clouds are stuck in the knuckles.

> The knuckles are like dinosaur humps. Our fingernails are like the sunset. Our hands are like cobwebs.

> The palm of my hand is like a tepee ...

Finally, a nursery child sat through assembly. When she stood up, she said to my fifteen-year-old son, who was on work experience in her school: 'My feet have gone fizzy'.

Lines like these are not great poems, or even good poems. Or maybe not even poems at all. Neither the writers nor their teachers claim any such thing. But they do have some of the components of poetry, and that is what this book is essentially about. It is concerned with the way children use poetic techniques (metaphor and simile in these examples) in order to learn. But most important, these lines are innocent of cliché, and there is nothing as important in good writing as the avoidance of hackneyed, worn-out phrases. That is why the Interlude later on is partly about that subject.

Stillman (1966: 119) tells us that 'a simile makes an explicit comparison between two things of a different kind or quality, usually introduced by "like" or "as"'. Eight-year-old Layla wrote the poem below, which is full of similes. Note how they start with the commonplace: indeed, the first line is a cliché. But then the writer's understanding grows under our eyes. This is the time to watch, to respect, to contemplate, to give serious and unremitting attention. Understanding, for the purpose of my comments about metaphor, is about how metaphor has to be fresh, not stale: dark oil and chocolate, not a rose. I print the poem here corrected. Its uncorrected form appears in chapter 11 (p 149):

My Mum smells like a rose.
My Dad's arm is like a smooth paper.
My Grandad's arm is like a rough pillow.
My Dad's eyes are like dark chocolate.
My Mum's hair is like dark oil.

....
Layla, 8

I believe (though you will have to take my word for it) that the lines about the darkness of chocolate and oil (defamiliarisations of eyes and hair, and also of chocolate and oil) are celebrations of a racial identity. They stem miraculously from a cliché. That rose is an easy image, familiar from chocolate boxes, songs and romantic poems. Of course, 'My love is like a red red rose'. But the progress in this poem from 'rose' to 'dark oil' is evidence of learning happening in the few minutes Layla was writing. This is a clear example of poetry's power to teach the writer about language. Layla teaches me here that clichés exist in two contrasting ways: they might simply be evidence of exhausted thought, or they might be evidence of the writer treading water as s/he prepares to swim. As we write the cliché, our mind may be preparing something fresher.

This writing is also (more importantly) a celebration of a daughter's love. But what is evident even to a reader who doesn't know Layla is that the phrases are also celebrations of language. Here St John's *logos* (the word) celebrates both our humanity in a basic, mystical sense, and also our humanity as users of a common medium that indeed makes us human: language. In recognising similarities between things (eyes and chocolate, hair and oil) Layla is making an important leap of the imagination without which poetry cannot exist.

'In metaphor' (Stillman continues) 'the comparison is implied, and one thing is said actually to be another or to function as another.' In the following examples, relating to the human body, the children are mostly using similes.

HANDS

Since this chapter is about writing poetry as a way of learning about the human body, we will look first at some similes for hands, spoken and then written by six-year-olds:

When we pull a fist it's like clouds are stuck in the knuckles.

The knuckles are like dinosaur humps.

Our fingernails are like the sunset.

Our hands are like cobwebs.

These examples show us how carefully children are prepared to look, and to give shape to expressions of what they see, as long as we give them time. We have to imprison them in the studying silence that all art, at one stage or another, requires. The clouds in the knuckles are the areas of bone from which the blood disappears when you tighten your hand. The dinosaur line shows how moments studying pictures of the stegosaurus have shed light in an unexpected place, suddenly, on the back of a writer's hand. The sunset is the pink colour, or it might refer to the little section of a circle at the bottom of our nails. It might, of course, be both. The cobwebs are the creases on our palms.

These similes were produced under pressure of intense questioning and longish silences (a minute in some cases): 'What do your knuckles look like? . . . What do they look like when you pull a fist? . . . What does the palm of your hand remind you of? Your nails?' . . . These lines are the work of children practising their craft. All children are poets, as Bin Ying (quoted in Hull 1988) says. To be a poet isn't to be a published writer, but to be someone concerned about learning, about finding his or her position in the world, that is reflected in what he or she writes. It is to be someone concerned with the daily necessity of getting the world provisionally right, so that s/he can work on it with a sound-looking and sound-sounding hypothesis. To be a poet is to work on first notes and drafts through the media of rhyme, rhythm, metaphor, simile and the rest.

This session with some six-year-olds was a useful one for working with simile and metaphor. I remember vividly an occasion when I came home from college. I was greeted by my father in his usual rather formal way with a handshake, and I noticed the nicotine stains and the little brown circles that I called 'toadmoles'. These have remained important images for me when I am thinking about my father. I comment in chapter 11, when I am discussing writing about love, that, if we want to write clearly and without a falsifying sentimentality about him or her, it helps to think about an object associated with the loved one. This is related to Eliot's 'objective correlative' (Gray 1984): an object, or a set of objects, that represents the emotions we feel. The nicotine stains and the toadmoles have made up an objective correlative for my feelings about my father in many a failed attempt at a poem about him.

I asked my friend Simon 'How old is so-and-so, do you think?' He told me what he thought and said 'I always look at people's hands when I'm thinking about their age'. Suddenly, hands became important symbols to me, if not as objective correlatives, but about our ageing. And, of course, hands are important to us in many other ways. Apart from their basic practical uses of holding and picking up and clutching, they symbolise lack of weapons and thus friendship; we hold each other's hands to protect and to express love; we wave them at sad moments of goodbye.

Children writing about hands will, obviously, write with a vigour that we associate with immediate experiences. As they look at and smell their hands, they come up with exhilarating similes. I asked these six-year-olds questions like:

- What do the palm of your hand/the knuckles/the thumb/the fingers remind you of?
- Can you smell your hand? What does it smell like?
- Clench your fist. What changes can you see as you do this, in shapes and colours?

and so on. Here is one example:

> The knuckles like big pale razor blade's.
> The nail's like pink almond shaped baby's finger's.
> And for the middle called a palm is the bark of a tree with deep cuts.
> Under neath bright pale tree sap.
> It feels smooth like a peach
> Skin with little bumps as hills.

....
Rachel, 10

This is a ten-year-old child learning. How can we talk about it? How can we reflect on it? What can we learn from it?

Look first at the punctuation inaccuracies. The child knows about possessive apostrophes, but hasn't distinguished them yet from plurals. But more importantly, she has spent time and intellectual energy looking, and forming metaphors to sharpen that looking. To put marks on her mistakes would be to force her emphasis to change from her looking, her learning, to what we might see as her clerical deficit. It would be to treat her as a potential office worker rather than as a present writer. This is, of course, to say nothing detrimental about office workers. But now in this child's life is the wrong time to be preparing her for such a role. Of course she needs to learn to punctuate correctly (though W H Auden never did). The time for that is when writing letters, and for communicating in other less charged ways than in the writing of poems. What might be more helpful is to show the child the strength the poem would take on if she used main verbs – and I did point this out. Here is her second draft:

> The knuckles are like big pale razor blade's.
> The nail's remind me of pink almond shaped baby's finger's.
> And the middle, called a palm, is the bark of a tree with deep cuts.
> Underneath is bright pale tree sap.
> It feels smooth like a peach
> There's skin with little bumps as hills.

> ....
> **Rachel, 10**

Here the piece has what we conventionally think of as correct grammatical shape, but the additions – mostly forms of the verb 'to be' – have added nothing to the images' vividness. The poem is still shapeless, but the metaphors have served a valuable purpose for the writer.

FEET

These children are following that ubiquitous topic 'Ourselves', and have moved on to the part about 'My body'. The teacher told me:

> They'd got the reference books, they'd got a CD ROM disk with information packed on to it, they'd got a cardboard skeleton from the museum, and I couldn't sleep one night and lay there and I thought suddenly, they're not using their own bodies! and the next morning I checked if they'd got any veruccas and no-one had and I told them to take a shoe and a sock off and to feel their feet, and then to look at it, the sole of it, and of course, because it was a first-hand experience the writing was very vivid, like this:

> Smooth soft skin, hard at the end, with curly whirly patterns on top. [Toes] like little marbles with a shiny coating . . .

> The sole reminds me of an arched bridge. It feels rough, like bricks. The lines on the sole look like pencil scribbles. The heel feels like a fist clenched together. It looks like a hardened nose. It reminds me of clay in a mould and looks like a finger gone numb. The toes look like mountains going into the distance. They look like cold baked beans.

> [The sole] feels like the finest sand and someone with a spade has run around and cut deep grooves in it. [The heel] feels like a boxing glove . . .

This teacher's story shows us how often we miss the obvious. Among all the books and posters and computers, all the things someone has a vested interest in making us buy – among all these is a cheap, free and far more vivid resource, our own bodies.

Also, one notices how the writing is not, in one sense of the word, finished. Sometimes the task of the writing is done when the notes are made. We needn't always even go on to a second draft. Here the children were being asked to re-acquaint themselves with their feet (they had all examined them many times, when they were very young); to engage in the first activity any artist and any scientist needs to engage in before doing anything else: they were being asked to observe.

The children were also free to draw. The teacher said to me (I was making notes after the lesson):

> I've long stopped dictating to children whether they should draw or write in response to a stimulus like this. I wanted them here to get into the early stages of observing and learning about their feet, and it's the lines they make, whether those lines are in words and sentences and paragraphs, or whether they're in drawings, it's those lines that'll help them learn. Someone, I've forgotten who, says that every line is a 'line into knowledge'. Is it Raphael? I like that. I feel it's true whether the lines are in a drawing or a piece of writing . . .

Obviously, this work will succeed with all parts of the human body. The next group of children were asked to feel their faces. They had closed their eyes because to eliminate one of the senses strengthens our use of the others. It simply does not matter that these metaphors and similes are not accurate in our eyes, anymore than a cartwheel in a PE lesson is less than perfect. These children are practising, and we have to praise their attempts just as we would praise their first cartwheels, when their legs flopped over and they landed in inelegant heaps.

My forehead feels
smooth as a drop of water
squidgy as a sponge

hot as five suns.

....
Jo, 7

My cheeks feel soft like the clouds
in the sky. Shine like the sun. bony like

a skeleton.
My nose feels soft like your clothes
My hair feels soft like a pillow

....
Claire, 6

MOUTH

Years ago I watched the poet/translator/historian Kevin Crossley-Holland teaching a class who were following a topic on the Anglo-Saxons. He drew on the blackboard a large mouth, and asked the children for some words to do with mouths. The first three words they came up with were 'tongue', 'teeth' and 'lips'. He wrote these words on the blackboard. He then nudged the children forward, and they came up with other words; fairly soon they started finding verbs, and then some adjectives. At one point, someone said 'kiss' (whether as a verb or noun is not recorded) and the children all laughed. Kevin Crossley-Holland wrote it on the board.

I have done this activity many times since in different ways, and am always struck by how children always produce nouns at the beginning of this activity. This is, first, because the word on the board was a noun, and, second, because tangible objects are always the first in children's consciousness: they are still Adam and Eve naming not only the beasts and trees, but also parts of their bodies, and the elements of the artificial world that surround them. This emphasis on nouns gives us, as teachers, the opportunity to talk about the power of verbs. The last time I did this activity, I divided the class (six-year-olds) into groups of five each, and suggested that each group elected someone who was fluent with the felt tips to be a scribe. Here are the contents of one of the sheets of paper they produced, re-organised later by me into nouns, verbs and adjectives:

> lips, teeth, gums, tongue, ulcers, toothache, fillings, bad breath, roof, ridges, tip, stringy bit,

> eat, drink, sip, slobber, gulp, gobble, roar, yell, shout, whisper, speak, kiss, be sick, vomit, hum, sing, murmur, mutter, suck, blow, snog,

> slimy, red, white, sharp, smooth, rough, cruel, smiling, frowning, laughing, grinning, yellow, lovely . . .

Also, there was the word 'slog'. What does that mean? I asked. 'It's the noise you make when you chew gum and your mum says "Stop slog-ging".'

A question arises from my sorting above. It is important to help children understand that many words can act as verbs, nouns and/or adjectives. 'Drink' and 'sip' from the list above are examples: both can be both noun and verb. It is best not to solidify our language into parts of speech. Instead, we must show children how the context in which words are used tells us about what part of speech that word is. My friend Andrea watched a lesson with ten-year-old children. The subject was adverbs, and, after explaining what an adverb was, and how it usually ended with '-ly', the teacher gave the children some examples: 'The boy ran to the park quick*ly* . . . I walked to the bank slow*ly* . . .' She asked for another example, and a boy offered 'The man ate his breakfast muesli . . .'

The children making the lists quoted above were learning something about the expansiveness of language; about how a moment's thought helps us see it grow in front of our mind's eye; they were also teaching the adults responsible for them about the power of their imaginations.

In the next example, seven- and eight-year-old children extended their work on their bodies by looking in their friends' eyes. This helped them to develop strong metaphors. I asked them questions: What shapes can you see? What colours? What do those shapes and colours remind you of? Can you add to that to make it clearer to me? All the following are short quotations from much longer pieces. Emily wrote:

> Hannah's eye looks like a swimming pool with a float in the middle . . . I see myself in her pupil . . .

The 'float in the middle' was a late addition under pressure from the question, 'Can you add to that to make it clearer to me?' She has captured the colours, both of the water and the eye, and also the shape of the pupil. And, come to that, of the float. It is as though the thought that went into the simile helps her learn about both sides of it.

This is true of Sally's line, too:

> My friend's eyelashes look like a feathery wall . . .

Mark is more direct, and makes a metaphor ('is' rather than 'like'):

> His eye is a sun of different colours . . . The pupil is a black hole, a black mirror . . .

Ashley demonstrates that children tell whatever seems to be the truth, however unpleasant it may sound to adults:

> I see me in her eye . . . the hazel in her eye reminds me of deep slime.

Hollie was Ashley's partner. She wrote:

> Ashley's eyebrows are like a caterpillar.

Tom gazed into his red-headed friend's eyes, and came up with:

> Chris's eyelashes look like a golden eagle's feather. His iris looks like the sea. His pupil looks like a cave, and his eyebrows are corn . . .

Benjamin's lines are simply beautiful in their exactness. He has indeed looked until it begins to hurt:

> My friend's eye colour is like a piece of wood on green glass. His eyelashes are like the wings of a lark.

As a postscript to writing about the body, here is an example of a writer, nine-year-old Daniel, writing lies about his knee:

> My left knee has a pair of hands.
> It sometimes eats frogs.
> It has a mouth the size of a hippo.
> It plays a little game of frisbee with the stars.
> When it is finished it goes for a swim
> with tissue paper in the toilet.
> It plays snooker when people go to the toilet, then

> SNAP

Perhaps human biology can stand as an example for learning in the other sciences. The body is there all the time. But children can examine animals dead and alive and write in the same kind of vivid way. They can watch chemicals reacting with each other, and ice melting in balloons. See, for an example of this idea, Sedgwick and Sedgwick (1996b) where four-year-olds work with ice and water to the empowerment of their language.

Chapter 3

'In the silences'

Learning more about living

That chapter about the body came first because the body is there to be felt, to be tasted, to be smelt, to be looked at, to be heard. The body is primary in a basic way: it is the subject of our initial first-hand experience. But what makes us human beings isn't our physicality. It is our language, and what we use it for. It is, indeed, our language that makes us unique. Those most precious words that embody our emotions speak to ourselves and our fellow humans about what we are.

ANGER

This next poem was written by an eleven-year-old in response to reading and listening to Vasco Popa's poem 'Just come to my mind' (to be found in Geoffrey Summerfield's anthology *Junior Voices, the Fourth Book* 1970):

Walk into my eyes
and the reflection will haunt you

Walk into my soul
and the sights will twist you

Walk by me
and the hatred will quiver you

Walk down my alley
and your blood will abandon you

Walk into a dark corner
and I will hunt you

Stay clear of me
or the evil will turn you

....
Ben, 11

A five-year-old writes, in response to the suggestion that she writes about what makes her feel angry:

When I was angry
I screamed and I
stamped my feet
and I scribbled
on the walls
I was quiet for
a long time.
I said sorry
that was all
right then
it was all
back to
together
again
the
end

....
Jenny, 5

That full stop at the end of line 7 is in a significant place, and should make us pause when we too readily decide to correct children's punctuation. It stands for the long silence the child experienced as she reflected on her anger and what had happened as a result of it. The lines 'that was all/ right then/ it was all/ back to/ together/ again' are a plea that this might be so, almost a prayer. The shape of the poem shows us that the child knows something about poems – that they vary in structure and so on – and I think it is best left as it is, a knife-shaped prayer.

Another five-year-old writes:

I stamped on my mum
I screamed in my mum's ear
I pulled my dad's tie
When my mum was exercises I
stood on my mums hair
I shouted in my mum's ear
I threw the ornaments
I smacked my mum around the face
I scribbled on my fridge

....

John, 5

An older child, of eleven years, has written this poem in his notebook:

Boiling face
go red
clench fists
forehead crinkles
mind goes blank
eyes water
stomach feels empty
feet go tense
grit teeth
see red
the way the Kurds
are being treated
Anger is
a voice yelling
rain falling heavily
on a car and bouncing up
sparks shooting out of eyes.

....

Daniel, 11

Four years after this boy wrote this poem, I asked him about it:

Mr L [his teacher] said, when you get angry, there's a certain point where you're beyond being angry . . . I can't remember much else . . . It's four years ago! Saddam Hussein was treating the Kurds like they weren't people, like they were animals . . .

We know plenty about children's tantrums and anger from our own adult point of view. This writer offers us an opportunity to explore the same subject from the child's angle. If I emphasise learning throughout this book, I want to make it clear that often that learning isn't only the child–writer's, but ours, too. Look, for example, how, in that last piece, the Kurds emerge out of some fairly conventional material: this boy has been looking at the papers, or listening to the radio, or watching television, with more attention than we, conventionally, might have expected.

Anger is most usefully approached using a strict form, because, of all the emotions, it is the one most likely to spill formlessly and embarrassingly on to the page. This eleven-year-old has used a form of a poem by Vasco Popa – the same one that Ben used (see p 41) (Summerfield 1970: 44):

> . . . See my eyes they're sparkling
> with black violence
>
> See my ears they're steaming
> like a caravan kettle
>
> See my tail is slashing like
> a circus whip
>
> See my mind it's dishing out
> words that you've never
> heard before . . .
>
> . . . .
> **Cara, 11**

Note how the suppression into a stanza shape has made the anger sound as if it is being expressed at great pressure; note how Cara used the image of the circus . . .

THE BOX

The box is a solemn and powerful way of getting children to contemplate their inner selves. I have written about it before (Sedgwick 1992: 110–30) in the context of drama. Here I want to look at it in a different light. Hannah was ten when she wrote this:

> My box is lined like ships of gold yet any other person would think it was old and scruffy and made from wasteful card. No my box is made from dreams, it sits there whispering. I wonder what's inside.
>
> I take my box to a special place under the stairs. When it's there it opens on its own. White streaks of silver glitter, then it goes back and there inside is my own favourite dream.
>
> Also in my box are three cold colours coughing and spluttering. In my box they're floating and fluttering in their own season according to the colour.
>
> In my box I have three specks of dust from the dusty dry paths of Hungary, not from the great tourist town, but from the hands of labourers.
>
> In my box there has been a great worry storm which has washed away my dream and place a nightmare and it's destroying my box.
>
> The lid of the box closes and it vanishes. The box was killed by the nightmare. The lid has slammed with the sound of cymbals.

Another girl wrote that 'in my box is the first word in the Hindu religion, which is "Om"'.

Teaching children about the box in their heads involves putting them in a prison of silence. It means persuading them to close their eyes, thus cutting out the most powerful of the senses, sight, in order to make their 'mind's eye' work. When I tell them that there is a box in each of their heads, they believe; when I tell them that the box in my head is made of 'jazz music, stained glass and the smell of frying onions' or 'the sound of my baby's laughter', they believe and understand. When I offer them the technique of alliteration, they understand it readily and use it, as in 'dust from the dusty dry paths'. When I ask them questions like 'How big is your box?' and 'What is its shape?' and 'What memories are in your box?' and 'How does your box close?' and 'How do you feel about your box closing?' they nod their heads reflectively, and write without question. The prison made of silence and open questions has set them free.

Asked about the beginnings of his poems, the Argentine writer Jorge Luis Borges said in an interview with Frank MacShane (MacShane 1973):

> I have to be attentive to what is about to happen . . . We must . . . let the Holy Ghost, or the Muse, or the subconscious – if you prefer modern

mythology – have its way with us . . . All this boils down to a simple statement: poetry is given to the poet

At readings, listeners sometimes ask poets where they get their inspiration from, and most poets reply that they don't wait for inspiration, that they try to write whenever they can; that if they waited for inspiration, they'd write even less than they do now. Jack London said somewhere, I recall, that he went after inspiration 'with a club'. Borges' remark quoted above seems to suggest that he did wait for inspiration – but the truth seems to be that inspiration comes mostly when the surface is primed by constant practice, constant thinking in rhythmical terms, constant attention to one's nerves. As Dunn *et al*. say (1987): 'You can't make it happen but you can make yourself open to its influence'.

The question for us as teachers of children trying to write poems is, how to get that surface primed. Henry is a friend of mine with a passion for poetry and what it can teach. We often share thoughts about it, and reactions to our work in the classroom. I watched as Henry worked with a group of ten-year-olds, using an autocratic way of getting them prepared for inspiration. First, he asked the children to close their eyes and cover them with their hands.

In the silences that we as teachers sometimes impose, objects are made on which the makers – the children, the writers – can reflect. I don't mean (it should be needless to say) silences imposed for mere disciplinary or administrative purposes. I mean those silences which set children free to think; thus reflecting on more than that object; reflecting, for example, happily or otherwise, on their world, and how the world is to them, and (who knows?) God. And this prison which I, the teacher, impose has become a kind of freedom for the child–writers. They have moved from the silence to God, and, in all likelihood, back again to the silence where somebody is writing. Silence and most oratory (like poetry and most oratory) are enemies. Oratory is not, pre-eminently, concerned with truth, but with a demagogic expression of a supposed certainty that is really a vested interest. Poetry, on the other hand, starts in the silence and reaches forward.

The poem might be given by 'the Holy Ghost, or the Muse, or the subconscious' as Borges puts it, tactfully taking in everyone – religious people, artistic people, even psychologists. In Henry's class the writing shows that children are facing up to their innermost characters, as they see what are the elementals with which they would fill a pristine world.

I have mentioned prayer and meditation, and much of this kind of work requires children to reflect prayerfully or meditatively on their own personalities. In the box exercise, they are building in this way a sort of extended metaphor for their own personalities. In the first example above, the writer is telling us that something she holds dear – her very personality, perhaps – may look 'old and scruffy' to the world, but to her it is made of 'gold . . . whispering dreams'. She is asserting her own worth in the face of potential rejection. It was during a session on this exercise that a girl told me that 'There is no box in my head'. I replied, after some thought, never having been told this before: 'That's your first line, then'. She looked at me for a moment, and expressionlessly wrote the line down. Later I went back and looked over her shoulder. She shifted her book so that I could read:

> . . . and if there was one it would be dark . . . everything in my box is hidden. In the dark corners there might be my family, I don't know for sure . . .

This child is spending valuable time and emotional energy exploring her own nature.

Henry is working with ten- and eleven-year-olds. He is talking, on the face of things, about the beginning of the world . . .

He asks the children to close their eyes and cover them up, and the children readily obey. I reflect for the umpteenth time how privileged we are to work with people who will do what must seem to them crazy things just because a teacher asks them to. Other things go through my mind while I watch this going on. I've shouted to classes in my time things like: 'Right! Silence!' or '4S, I want your complete attention . . . NOW!' and then expected them to write poetry.

I also noticed that the children already had pens, pencils and writing paper in front of them as the teacher talked. This is obvious, of course, but there have been times in my experience when the teacher does an admirable job of pumping the classroom atmosphere – before s/he supplies the children with what they need practically. This allows the air to hiss wastefully out of the tyre *before they get started* as the children rush to drawers and trays to get what they need. Something else that causes that escaping hiss is the administrative task of writing the date, name, margin etc. Poets do date their work, of course; and sign it; and make it look neat – but afterwards.

When the room is silent, Henry says:

> You are going on a journey to the very beginning of the world. The earth is only half an hour old, and you are the only being in it. There's just you and a clean, fresh mist, and you are walking through the mist on your own. Then three colours shine out of the mist. What are they? Quickly, write down the three colours that you see at the very beginning of the world.

> Now, add a word, an adjective, to each of the colours to tell us what kind of, say, red it is.

Close your eyes again. As you walk along through the mist with those three colours, you hear three sounds from the first hour in the life of the world. What sounds are they? (the children write). Now three very pure smells (they write again).

Now you come across two objects. One's a surprise – what is that doing there on the first morning in the history of the world? The other isn't a surprise at all. What are they?

Now you see a signpost pointing to the horizon. What's there on the horizon? That's where you have to go.

Now read your notes over, carefully. Add words here and there – make the colour more clear, for example, or add adjectives to the sounds and the smells to make them clearer to the reader – who is, at the moment, yourself, of course. You have got a first draft of a poem about a very strange world that you have created yourself, in your imagination.

At this point, Henry asked the children if anyone would like to read their notes to the class – twice. The first time, he listened, going so far as to over-act listening. The second time, he interrupted with questions: 'What animals were they? What kind of tree was it? What kind of house was it on the horizon?'

Paul read out his notes. After the questioning, they looked like this:

red, scarlet   Ting
yellow, light   ding
blue, sky   bing

flower, bluebell (crossed out) rose   sing, bird, blackbird
tree, oak   shing sun   gorrila
                          gorilla   shining
water, sea twirling   shineing   shining

....
Paul, 10

The words Paul added to his original were 'bluebell', 'rose', 'blackbird', 'gorilla', 'oak', 'shining' (variously spelt).

Linzi's first draft (1) looks very rough:

what the
world could
be like   green > lime
                 blue . sky   people walking
                 red roses   bones lying on
                                        the floor

                 dogs
                     crying   bubbling
         car crash   water
              bang bomb

    opemin
parthyome
        flowers   peach rose
skacking drinking water

There are many heavy crossings out on this piece of A4, as well as a curving snake-like design at the bottom. This took about ten or fifteen minutes under pressure of the questioning described above. Her second draft (2) read:

What the world could be like

The smell of lime was coming into the open air,
Blue sky flying over us,
red roses going backwards and forwards,
Dogs crying louder and louder,
suddenly a car crash into a brick wall,
Then there was bang it was a bomb.
There was a lovely smell of opium.
The fresh smell was a peach rose,
sparkling water running down the steam.
The people are trying to walk but they can't
At the end of the world bones lying ever way
and the bubbly water going all over

Her third draft (3) differed significantly in some respects:

What the world could be like

The smell of lime coming into the open air,
Blue sky flying over us,
Red roses going backwards and forwards,
Dogs crying louder and louder,
There was a lovely smell of opium.
There was a lovely row of peach roses.
Suddenly a car was going so bad that it crashed,
Then a bomb landed Bang!!!,
All the people was trying to walk but
they couldn't.
At the end of the world there was bones everywhere,
The sparkling bubbly water went over everything,
the world was ended.

I want to make two points about this piece of work. First, while Henry's introduction and instructions invited writing about freshness and beauty, this writer has gone beyond that to her own current obsessions. And they are entirely understandable as obsessions in the world we live in, and in its portrayal on television and in newspapers and magazines: drugs, violent death. There is still a tendency to sentimentalise childhood, evident, for instance, in some poetry written for children and in much material produced commercially for nurseries. At times like this, child–writers have the chance to correct our images. This isn't to see children as unpleasant or dark-minded; merely as distressed as we adults are by the 'slings and arrows' and 'The heartache and the thousand natural shocks/ That flesh is heir to . . .' (Hamlet, 3. i).

Second, the process the writer went through is one that some children never experience. And yet look at the evidence for learning this has provided us with. From the bones of (1) to the muscle of (3), Linzi has toyed with words, played with them, accepted them, rejected them. It simply does not matter that she has not produced an entirely 'good' poem. We do not need, as teachers, for her sake, to be waving around what Scannell (1977: 74) scornfully calls 'marvellous "poems"' written by children. We might do that for our own sake, and our self-esteem, or our esteem among our colleagues. But what we can see here is the progress to some excellent, chilling touches – the 'sparkling bubbly water over everything' for example, and the nightmare about the injured people 'trying to walk but/ they couldn't'. This is a child making a poem, an object that will help her reflect on her fears. She has had a relatively unusual opportunity, and she has taken it with gusto.

Sometimes, the children's first drafts were stronger than their later drafts because those first words were so bare. Some writers prettified their poems. 'I hear the sweet cheep of the bluebirds / I see them lovingly peck the candytufts' wrote one girl, identified, rightly I suspect, as the most gifted writer in the group. But despite her use of unusual words ('crystalline water . . . candytuft flowers') her work became conventional as she worked on. Paul, however, stayed bare and odd:

> Ting ding bing,
> There's a blackbird singing.
> The bright yellow shining sun
> Makes a shadow of the oak tree.
> There's a sky blue twirling ocean
> with rocks on the sand below,
> scarlet red roses,
> other flowers nearby,
> an angry gorilla coming towards me.
>
> ....
> **Paul, 10**

Claire, who was eleven, wrote:

> The first mother
> Pulled the first
> Silly faces
> And the baby laughed . . .
>
> On the path
> I saw an apple
> And took a bite.
> My hunger was cured forever.

Most of the children showed some experimental interest. Lee, for example, broke a traditional rule by beginning 'And a river meandering . . .' Another example: this eleven-year-old boy's first draft was lost. His poem finished up, in its final draft, as follows:

The Dawn

Time
has begun.
A watery blue haze
shines on an immaculate
landscape. Deep purple emptiness
threatens the bright violet on the edge of
the void. The smouldering rock poises to fight
the scent of the newly-born salt-water.

Life
has begun.
The loud thunder
signals it. Happy voices
sing, the clammy air rejoices
and changes darkness to light. Water
rushes to and fro, feeding life. A shout of laughter
appeals for more.

....
Andrew, 11

'The loud thunder/ signals it . . . Deep purple emptiness/ threatens the bright violet on the edge of/ the void . . . A shout of laughter/ appeals for more . . .' The first thing that strikes me about this poem now, two years after it was written, is that those sentences are so direct. There is no passive mode. 'It is signalled by the loud thunder . . . the bright violet is threatened by the deep purple emptiness . . .' The passive mode is used by many writers trying to compose their early poems, because, I suspect, it delays the action. It is less committing. In a similar way, the 'ing' form of verbs, the present participle, has a delaying function. Perhaps the overuse of adjectives has the same function. In this brief poem we have 'watery', 'blue', 'immaculate', 'deep', 'purple', 'bright', 'smouldering', 'newly-born', 'loud', 'happy' and 'clammy': eleven adjectives in a poem of 71 words.

And yet the poem has a strength. Why? I wrote to Andrew two years after he had written it as an eleven-year-old, and talked to him about his poem. I note here that Andrew hasn't thought about his poem since he wrote it; that he doesn't, normally, consider drafting; and that he is concerned about shape. He said:

The shape is like that because it builds it up, it builds an atmosphere. Each step builds an atmosphere. I like it like, it keeps an order. It starts again at 'Life' because the poem is about two different things, life and time. The beginning of time, and the beginning of life. I haven't thought about it since I wrote it, till I got your letter. Looking at it now, I still think it builds up an atmosphere . . . There's a certain sense of regularity and tension. I made those line changes because I wanted it to be like a PA system, a voice overheard as a PA system: 'TIME (long pause) HAS BEGUN . . .' That pause after 'Time' dictated the rest of the poem . . . It was a first draft, I don't think I'd change it . . .

Something similar is happening in a different way in this poem. The ten-year-old boy who wrote it was subject to terrifying tantrums, and this behaviour was, of course, unacceptable in all the main places where he spent his time: home, the games field, the classroom. He was a boy with severe emotional problems, and here poetry breaks into his life and satisfies a special emotional need:

I feared more than those
    bizarre animals
       those mysterious
          sounds
were
        unfriendly

They were foul mouthed
    and they
       glanced at me
      wildly

They wore fragments
    of torn velvet

I was invisible through the remote lakes

I was trying to act scarce

This poem bears examination. It was written with a stimulus from Sandy Brownjohn (1982), who in turn got the idea from Vernon Scannell. Following their examples, I had made a prose version of Stephen Spender's famous poem 'My parents kept me from children who were rough' (Gibson and Wilson 1965: 71) and asked the boy to make a poem from this data. What he wrote bears very little resemblance to either my clumsy prose or to Spender's verse, because after the initial stimulus his work fragments into broken images that make it look like some piece of an ancient language of which occasional phrases and sentences only have survived. If we, as teachers, were to tidy this piece up, we would be making a serious mistake, because to respect the boy's personality and feeling, and to empathise with him and his emotions, is to recognise at least that this fragmentation is part of the message. And, as Roland Barthes says (1982: 3): 'Incoherence [is] preferable to a distorting order'.

Several of the images (which bear no relation to anything in Spender's poem) such as 'fragments/of torn velvet' and the 'remote lakes' are mysterious, even impenetrable, and mystery and impenetrability are stages every poet must go through. Even the grammar is obscure (what did he fear more than the 'bizarre animals'? Or did he fear the animals more than whatever 'those' stands for? And why 'through' in the penultimate line, when 'under ' or 'beneath' or 'across' would make sense and clarify?) But look how he takes the cliché 'act scarce' and makes it fresh and vivid. The lack of punctuation has a role here, and if we plaster the paper with red marks, we must be aware of what we are doing: training a secretary rather than teaching a writer.

Images of boxes, of beginnings, or religious activities like prayer figure largely in this work because we are looking for what is contained within our nature and we are going back to a kind of basic. This next section is about a little prison cell that sets children terribly free. The cell is a stanza from Wes Magee's poem 'Good Questions, Bad Answers' from his collection *Morning Break* (Magee 1988). I can convey the shape of this poem by saying that each stanza is built like this:

> Where was my mum
> when I needed her
> when I was two
>   At a party.

> Where's the friend
> I played with every day
> when I was five?
> Committed suicide in Scotland.

There is in the writing of poetry always a possibility of subversion, of young writers saying what in polite company would be the unsayable.

This is probably true of poetry in a way it can't be true of any other kind of writing. This girl wrote these lines recalling a horrible moment from her childhood. As she writes it, and looks at it, and reflects on it, she moves constantly but gradually closer to coming to terms with the event that inspired it, and also to losing her mother finally and entirely one terrible day. The boy who wrote the second stanza recalls an even more terrible time.

A nine-year-old girl wrote this, and proudly read it to the whole year in her middle school:

> Where's the baby
> that was in my mum's tummy
> when she was thirty-one?
> Standing here.

Other children use different structures for examining their lives. One is the three-line stanza 'I used to be . . ./ but/ now I'm . . .' which often leads away from the simple ('I used to be six /but/ now I'm seven') to the confidence-asserting ('I used to be rubbish at swimming/ but/ now I'm in the gala'), the surreal ('I used to dance on Mercury /but/ now I dance on the rings of Saturn') and the wittily punning ('I used to tap-dance/ but/ then I fell in the sink'). Another useful liberating prison cell is 'I don't like to boast/but/ . . .' as in this oddity:

> I don't like to boast
> but
> Pamela Anderson is buying me underwear for Christmas.

> ....
> **Michael, 8**

Here are two more examples:

> I don't like to blow my own trumpet
> but
> I just parted the Red Sea like Moses.

> ....
> **Sally, 8**

I don't like to brag
but
I've been to the other side of the other side of the universe.

....
Richard, 11

A French teacher told her class that the French equivalent of blowing one's own trumpet was sending flowers to oneself, and a child wrote with self-deprecating wit:

I don't want to send flowers to myself
but
no-one else will.

....
Melanie, 9

Children learn about themselves through the writing of poetry. They can examine their own bodies, hands, feet, eyes, brows; they can reflect on what their six favourite words are. They can look at, or dream up, or reflect on a box in their heads; they can (exposing their fantasies) lie, and they can boast. They can meditate on their emotions. They probably, at times, need to be quiet for 'a long, long time'. They can reflect, almost prayerfully, and at least meditatively, on what the beginning of their perfect worlds might be like. They can reflect on their autobiographies. But also, they can learn about their world. And that is what the next part is about.

But first, an interlude about two critical issues for the teacher of poetry – whatever the children are writing about.

An interlude

Two central issues: clichés and drafting

Why have I linked these two issues? Because we nearly all have a tendency to think and write in clichés. Our first draft, of a thought, of the expression of a feeling, of an application letter, of a poem, will always have hackneyed, tired phrases in it, because it is hard enough work to get started let alone worry about freshness. Later, as we become owners of a second draft on which we can reflect, we can see those phrases for what they are, and cut them away, or change them. We can't act on a text until we have one. But the first draft will be the first of two, or of several, or of many, the total number depending, at least in part, on the importance of the final product.

CLICHÉS

Simile and metaphor are central to poetry, of course, but also to everyday speech. The crucial difference is that most similes and metaphors in daily use are also clichés, such as 'he ran away like a scalded cat' or 'I'm over the moon'. On the radio news this morning, a reporter told us that 'stories about Hindu gods drinking milk were *spreading like wildfire*' (my italics). A cliché is a phrase, or word, or comparison that has been overused to the point where it is simply tedious. 'Scalded cat' was once a vivid description of a response to a frightening moment, because we can have no doubt that a cat suddenly hit by boiling water will move fast; 'over the moon' conveyed excellently pleasurable, heady excitement; and news spreading 'like wildfire' encapsulated perfectly, the first time someone said it, the speed gossip takes on. But now, if someone used any of these phrases in a poem, except with irony, we would know they were writing when more than half asleep.

Because of the enormous speed and power of communication, clichés plummet from being fresh ways of saying things to hackneyed uselessness within a few weeks. 'Economical with the truth', for example, was a slyly witty way of hiding prevarication, for a few minutes after someone had said it. Days later, with its exposure throughout the English-speaking world in newspapers and television, it was a cliché. Something similar happened with the American phrase 'dead in the water'. It was a disturbing way of describing a hopeless political position once. But use it now in serious writing, and we can tell that the user has shrugged shoulders and given up thinking any further on the matter.

But it has to be said that the cliché is the sworn enemy (there's one!) of poetry, simply because a cliché's familiarity makes it almost impossible for us to see clearly what the writer is saying. 'Sworn' once added immeasurable strength to the notion of enmity because of the power oaths once had. Now an oath is rarely more than a swearword, and 'sworn' is at best a weak intensifier. Clichés are evidence of the user's desensitisation to language, especially when they are used without any understanding of the original metaphor. A sports reporter has just said on the radio that one football club 'are firmly rooted at the top of the table', forcing the question: how can anything be *rooted* at the *top* of anything else? To be unaware of meanings and nuances like this is to disempower ourselves and our language.

That is why we discourage children from writing 'pretty' with reference to flowers, or 'nice' in reference to smells. In fact, children are better at avoiding clichés than adults, partly for the obvious reason that they have fewer clichés in their wordhoard (Saxon, I reckon, for 'database') than we have, but also because they dread getting things wrong. But we can still usefully teach them the game of cliché-hunting; and this is often done best through the activity I have described elsewhere as 'editing friends'.

The traditional English poem that follows was once a poem composed of similes. The purpose of these similes was to make the world strange, so that we could look at it in a new way. No doubt it survived as a lively poem longer than it would have done today, because it didn't have to co-exist (as it does now) with instantaneous mass-communication. To us it is a useful example of tired phrases, of clichés:

> As wet as a fish, as dry as a bone,
> As live as a bird, as dead as a stone,
> As plump as a partridge, as poor as a rat,
> As strong as a horse, as weak as a cat,
> As hard as flint, as soft as a mole,
> As white as a lily, as black as coal,
> As plain as a pike-staff, as rough as a bear,
> As tight as a drum, as free as the air,
> As heavy as lead, as light as a feather,
> As steady as time, uncertain as weather.

Here, 'dry as a bone', 'strong as a horse', 'black as coal', 'plain as a pike-staff', 'free as the air' and 'light as a feather' have all attained the status of cliché.

Metaphor and simile in poetry can never be clichés, because they are there to enhance, to clarify, to make vivid, not to dull and obscure. Some teachers encourage cliché with notices in classrooms listing 'Good ways to begin a story: "Once upon a time" . . . "once there was . . ."' I think that the cliché is linked to the template. The latter is not simply a physical object used in art lessons where the teacher imposes his/her view of an object on the child. It is a metaphor for what schooling, as opposed to education, is: the placing down on a child's life of a view of how things ought to be. The cliché and the template have, in other words, political implications. In using them, the teacher insists on an old way. S/He controls. The cliché controls our thought as the cardboard template does our pencil; as structured play does our play.

Lack of cliché is the only one indispensable condition of poetry that I know. It is not enough to be free of the hackneyed phrase, the literal template. But it is the start. And it begins in the conviction that all important writing involves more than one draft. For some vigorous, fresh phrases, note these similes for jelly thought up by a class of five- and six-year-olds:

It's sticky, like red pop, like blood in a bowl, a red swimming pool it's stretchy like a pair of pants when you stretch them, soft like a sponge, squidgy like a flannel, stretchy like elastic bands, sticky like chewing gum, squashy like doughnuts, like a balloon, it wobbles in the mouth, it's like a trampoline, it's bouncy like a bouncy castle. When the spoon sticks in it, it makes a crack in the jelly . . .

DRAFTING

Drafting is a process by which, first, the writer learns more about what s/he is trying to say, and, second, learns to say it with greater clarity, elegance and balance. It is not the process in two leaps from first attempt to 'fair copy'. Even though writing is a working *process*, the *product*-oriented approach to teaching it survives. For too many teachers, it's got to look good or, in the jargon of what a friend of mine calls the 'hessian movement', 'aesthetically pleasing'. For example, after years of insisting that 'there's a better word than "nice"' a teacher tells a child that 'it isn't clever to write too much' as he prepares his production line, moving from initial writing ideas to double-mounted candidates for a 'nice' display within a couple of hours. His anxiety was mainly with his concerns over his workload as trimmer and mounter.

It is unfair and pointless to ask a child to keep rewriting his/her work out until it is perfect. Simply copying and copying is a drudgery that 16th-century monks suffered, and there is no need (not to mention time) for it now. It is merely a way of controlling children, and evidence of a teacher's need for immaculate presentation rather than learning. To see how useless a process it is, watch a child doing it and try to make a mental list of what s/he is learning. Children (and, indeed, all writers) need to be freed from the tyranny of the fair copy. If we are more concerned with neat italic handwriting and coloured borders than with the process of learning through which the child is going by writing, we are selling both the child and the art short. We are teaching him or her to be a compliant clerk rather than an independent creative learner, and treating the art as a means to ignoble end.

The fair copy is, essentially, a giving up. As the French writer Paul Valéry said, 'a poem is never finished, only abandoned' (quoted in Auden 1971: 423). It represents the best we can do after all the intellectual and emotional energy we have brought to bear on the task. I often say that the look of a poem on the page is important; by this I mean its shape, and the relationship, tense or relaxed, between the meanings on the one hand, and the stanza and line-endings on the other. I am not concerned with the crayoned border round the edges or, worse, the shading that often obscures the words of the poem.

How should children learn about the drafting process?

It is probably best for children to work on large sheets of cheap paper, such as newsprint, with a pencil that's trained not to mind crossing out, scribbling and doodling. Using cheap paper teaches them that making mistakes isn't a serious matter: writing on expensive paper, it could be argued, discourages experiment. At least three drafts can take place on the same sheet of paper. Children must make their second, at least, on top of their first, by using arrows and asterisks, to show where new words and phrases are to be inserted, and by using oblique lines (/) in places where, on reflection and after reading their drafts aloud, they decide they want line breaks. Double slashes (//) are for stanza breaks. They should be discouraged from using erasers, because they are strategies for avoiding work, and often what is rubbed out is needed later. They should be taught not to confuse the secretarial with the compositional. When a child has written, for example, about the birth of a new sister or brother, it is inappropriate for her or him to worry about punctuation and spelling because s/he has fully expressed her or his rejoicing.

Second, children can make creative use of word processors. These, increasingly common in schools, are all too often used for presentation. This is a mistake: the flexibility and speed of a good word processor is useful for encouraging experiment in the content and order of writing. They are therefore useful for the earlier stages of composition. While I was working on this book, I printed it out several times. This is partly because working on paper with a pen is different from working on a screen. It throws up different problems. For example, on a screen I tend to miss repetitions over a chapter, or even over the whole typescript, because I can only see one page at a time. Also, copy on the screen always looks neat, and this means that the eye tends to drift over it uncritically. It is necessary, for me anyway, to dig in at my material with a pencil. Again, I print out my script several times because I pass my work-in-progress round to friends with interests like mine for their comments. Critically, in early drafts I allow myself clichés, to capture an idea that is only on the edge of my consciousness, because if I don't write something down, I might lose it.

There are more than two ways to compose drafts. There is pencil/pen and paper, of course; there is the word processor. But children can also dictate their words to an adult, or to a tape recorder or Dictaphone.

On one occasion, I showed a spectacularly messy page to a class of eight-year-old children who were used to drafting. On the back wall of their classroom was a large display divided into three. The first third was marked 'first draft', the second, 'reflection' and the third 'final copy'. Large cut-out arrows dived from one to two to three. This was too programmatic and over-simplified for most writers' experience of the process of composing. Every writer knows, whether his or her writing has been the making of careful letters of application, or whether it has been the construction of novels, that things are by no means as simple as this. But this display was an improvement on what I used to practise as a young teacher. I expected a perfect, neat copy first time, every time.

It is also an improvement on classrooms where teachers expect sound spelling at every stage in the first draft. To that end, every child is supplied with a 'word book', or a 'vocabulary book', and has to present this to the teacher open at the relevant page of the alphabet whenever he or she is uncertain about the spelling of a word. This presents many problems. 'How do you spell "mong"?' says someone, book open at 'M', 'a' already written down in her exercise book. A child said to me yesterday: 'Can I have "because"? I don't know, I might already have it'. And which teacher pretends that all the words in a word book at the end of a school year have all been learnt? Bad spelling resembles cliché in one way: they are both methods of getting something down before it is lost. If you can't (and I can't) spell buddleia for sure, you write buddl- and a squiggle, and remember to look it up, much as you write the cliché that has a rough shape of the idea in your head. Both will have to do, for the time being.

But the relatively sophisticated children in this school didn't have word books. They were allowed to try words, making a mental note to check them later. They did what experienced writers do when faced with a spelling problem: they kept going. They were familiar with the drafting display at the back of the room.

Nevertheless, these children were still appalled at my messy page. I asked them, did they like the look of this page? And in unison they said

read my mind

You're taken my food away ~~for~~
Come closer to me.

See my teeth there as *sp* ~~hard~~ *sharp*
as thorns

See *my* claws they claw up with
anger

See my eyes their sparkiing with
violence

See my ears their steaming like
a keetle

See my tail its slashing like
a whip

See my mind its dishing out
words

don't eat my words or I'll
eat yours.

by
cara

Abbott

Figure 1 First draft

read my mind

You've taken my food away
trampel closer to me.

See my teeth their as sharp
as a pine tree.

See my claws they claw up
with pointed anger

See my eyes their sparkling
with black ~~anger~~ violence

See my ears their steaming like
a caravan kettle

See my tail its slashing like
a circus whip

See my mind its dishing out
words that you've never
heard before

don't eat ~~it~~ my golden words
or ill eat yours.

Second draft

by cara
Abbott
Tattingstone School
19/6/96

Figure 2 Second draft

Read my Mind

You've taken my food away,
trample closer to me.

See my teeth, they're as sharp
as a pine tree.

See my claws. They claw up
with pointed anger.

See my ears. They're steaming like
a caravan kettle.

See my tail. It's slashing like
a circus whip.

See my mind. It's dishing out
words that you've never
heard before.

Don't eat my golden words
or I'll eat yours.

Cara 21 June 1996 third draft

Figure 3 Final copy

that they did not. It 'wasn't very neat'. There were 'too many crossings-out'. It didn't look 'very nice' . . . Why was there this negative reaction to drafting? The answer is obvious.

Children react against what I would see as the necessary mess of the poem in progress because the rest of our teacherly rhetoric is about getting things done, finishing on time, and on presentation skills.

We might usefully display children's work today, with a first messy scribbled-on draft, and an arrow leading to a second draft; along that arrow we might write words like 'thought', 'reflection'; 'discussion'. We might end with an arrow leading to a publication, which could be a typed-up sheet, a neatly-written 'fair copy' – but even this should concede the 'provisionality' of such a stage. A poem isn't finished, just jacked in, packed up. Shrugged away.

As I write I have on my desk copies of the worksheets of Philip Larkin's poem 'At Grass', printed in *Phoenix* (Larkin 1974). The poem itself is published in Larkin's *Collected Poems* (1988). Two things strike me about these pages. One is the extraordinarily methodical approach. Larkin is always tidy in his task. First, he writes down the opening stanza. The first three lines will stay as they are, and the form of the stanza – its metre – is already decided. Then he slashes through the final two lines, and copies the stanza out again. By the end of the second copying, Larkin has his rhyme scheme intact (though not the rhyme with which he will finally end this stanza). In this careful, painstaking way he progresses through the poem.

But in contrast to this, the slashings and crossings-out become more and more vigorous. He hacks false starts through with thick black lines, and scrawls diagonals through already scribbled on lines. Marginal notes suggest different options here and there. This suggests that even a painstaking, formal poet like Larkin (at least in this poem) needs the romantic scribble, the passionate hack, the desperate scrawl through words.

The most exciting sight of a new poem is often the messy early drafts, where we can see the poet thinking. The same is true of children: they need to understand that those early pieces of paper, slashed with crossings-out, surrounded with arrows saying 'I should've put that there, and this here' and filled up marginally with new ideas – those pieces of paper are vital in the pristine sense of that word. They are the life blood of their learning and their poetry, whether that learning is about themselves, as it was in the first part of this book, or about the world around them, as in the next.

Part II

Chapter 4

Introduction

A fresh look at the world

Before that interlude, I tried to show how children learn about themselves – their bodies, their feelings, their lives, their relationships – by what we might call the training of the imagination: the education of what Coleridge (1907) sees as the fusing of 'synthetic and magical power'. My interlude was an attempt at frying some garlic: what it said must affect everything I write, much as garlic affects everything in a dish. In the poems children compose, we need to detect a taste of the awareness of what cliché is and a strenuous avoidance of it, and the presence of the kind of contemplation that goes into the making of drafts. Children need to keep in their minds all the time they are writing the need to find *the phrase that hasn't been found before*. They must develop the will to work on their early notes as if they mattered (because they do): to draft.

The aim of this next part is to demonstrate ways in which children can learn about the world around them through the making of poems. Science, geography, history and religious education are my interests here. But before I discuss them, I must say that writing involves, perhaps most of all, learning about language. And that learning is something that runs (killing clichés and making drafts are two of its appearances) throughout this book. We learn about language, not by having skills exposed and addressed in a hierarchical manner, but by using it. Everyone is learning about language as soon as s/he looks out from his/her cot and wonders. It is a false picture to insist that older children must, say, write their name in neat joined-up script before they can move on to creating their own sentences.

So, two central points. First, children can't study science, religion, geography or history without using language. The child tussles with the words that might reflect in some way what s/he means. And second, that tussle is a tussle with language as well as with the subject the child is writing about. Learning and language are bound up together, and any effort to disentangle them would be beside the point. That learning includes secretarial skills. Children learn best how to make correct sentences by making them to some purpose. That includes main verbs, subjects, predicates and full stops. They learn what adjectives and adverbs are by using them, not by being told what they are. And all this happens better with poetry than with prose, because it is intensive. What a child uses in a poem (if it is a real poem, authentic in terms of his or her feelings, and recognising the demands of form) stays used. It matters, and becomes part of the child's tools.

Using language to learn about the world should be the least troublesome part of this book. Learning about everything around us – here, now, then, there – is what everyone (possibly without thinking about it very much) agrees children in schools should be doing. The world is, after all, first of all, the face of things. For both the most reactionary representative of the back-to-basics movement and the most adventurous teacher, education and schooling deal with the world. That means science, history, geography, technology, sociology, religious studies, as well as all the arts that readers of a book like this will, I hope, take for granted.

Two difficulties arise. The first appears when one reflects on how subjective any view of the world is. Some politicians don't understand that learning about kings and queens is learning about a certain view of history, and a very powerful one too. And that power stems in large part from our not understanding this deep subjectivity; not understanding that an insistence on teaching stories about, say, Queen Victoria's marriage means not teaching something else: possibly about the lives of London's poor. Also, being 'fundamentalist' about education (to quote a politician talking during the week in which I write the first draft of this), and therefore supporting what he called the 'basics', is to be subjective; is to see the future of certain children in a very specific way: as clerks, at best. And clerks, indeed, in outdated offices, without the benefits of computers and spell checks and other aids to writing, that will, like it or not, make much of what passes for 'basic education' in British political debate irrelevant.

Unlike those politicians who sail their views (and indeed their information) under the dubious convenience flags of 'common sense' and 'what every parent wants', I am happy to confess my subjectivity. I require of the education system that it helps children to be independent learners, to be not only inheritors of their culture but critics of it. I want them to be able to manipulate all the tools a broad curriculum offers them to learn about the world; I want them to 'have life, and . . . have it more abundantly' (John 10:10). This involves, above all else, the imagination, that weird power that makes discordant things collide, for example, in metaphor; that harmonises what Coleridge calls the 'general and the concrete'.

To want children prepared as clerks is equally subjective. To treat the world as if it were, indeed, the unquestioned, and unquestionable, face of things is not to go very far educationally. It is one of our tasks as teachers and learners to go beneath surfaces. To be what the same politician called a 'fundamentalist' about education, always talking about the 'basics', is to see the world entirely as a surface, and our relationships with it and each other in a mechanistic and simplistic way.

The second difficulty arises with that distinction I've made between schooling and education. While schooling doesn't preclude education, education does preclude the kind of schooling that is no more than socialisation. Schooling merely inducts children into a powerful, constructed world-view, while education, in the course of that induction, sows the seeds of critical enquiry. The educated person can make his or her synthesis between the known and the accepted, on the one hand, and the to-be-discovered, on the other. Education is a great deal more than the making of compliant individuals for a commercial culture.

The schooled person, in contrast, is merely trained to carry on as the race has carried on before. If we prepare children for the workplaces of industry, we will be preparing them for a world that will no longer exist by the time they come to inhabit it. A manager of a light engineering firm once chilled me by saying that teaching was merely 'a routine batch exercise'. Nothing has done more to blur the education/schooling distinction than the metaphor of the market: the notion of delivering services. A routine batch exercise, or a conscientious celebration of our humanity through writing: nothing could put into stronger relief than that opposition the contrast between the teacher's necessary humanism, and the mechanics of the market, with its routine batches, which become cruel when applied to human beings.

And that brings me back to my earlier sentence above – 'learning about the world is what everyone agrees children in schools should be doing'. The learning is not only vital for the children. All adults working with children should be open to new understandings of the world. 'Delivery' (from one to another) is the wrong metaphor because if a teacher (meaning any adult working with children) is not a learner, there is a strong chance that a child isn't either. And the teacher who is a learner cannot be seen as a hired hand of the state, merely delivering received wisdom.

The writing of poetry subverts, or attempts to subvert, the idea of the child as a passive receiver of the tradition, and of what a given politician sees as the 'basics'. What is infinitely more important is that we should help children look intensely at their world, like ten-year-old Barnaby, who has read Miroslav Holub's poem 'The Door' (in Summerfield 1970). This shows that anything that can be opened – doors, windows, chests, drawers, fridges, cupboards – can be a stimulus, if children are freed to imagine what they like, especially the impossible:

> Run over there to open the window
> maybe there will be
> a bush
> a field of animals

a secret place
in the sunshine

Run over there to open the window
maybe there will be
a cat chasing
a nose sniffing
or a gate
talking in the daylight

Run over there to open the window
maybe there will be
a storm but it won't stay

Run over there to open the window
even if the pine is falling
even if there's a window fighting
even if there's a tree wishing

at least
there will be
a breeze
left in the air

....
Barnaby, 10

Writing about the world can sharpen the focus powerfully. It requires a different angle from the conventional one to get rid of the clichés, to make sparks jump. One way in which children can do this is by becoming, for an hour, Martians.

Chapter 5

Martians, Riddles and Snapshots

MARTIANS

In 1979 a collection of poems appeared called *A Martian Sends a Postcard Home*. The poet, Craig Raine, was the most prominent writer in a loose group whose style was called 'Martian' by James Fenton. The title poem of the book (Raine 1979: 1–2) is composed of a series of observations of the world and various objects in it – books, mist, rain, cars, watches, telephones, lavatories – not *looked at* by someone whose vision is jaded by much casual, unfocused looking, for whom 'the vision splendid . . . [has faded] into the light of common day', but *seen* as though the observer had never seen them before; as though s/he were a Martian; as though, we might say, s/he had an innocent eye, or what Neil Corcoran (1993: 235) calls a 'cleansed perception', an 'unprejudiced observation'.

There are potent possibilities in this for children's poetry writing. Young writers, to a greater or lesser extent, already have this way of seeing things: they come, as Wordsworth says, in the poem quoted in the last paragraph, trailing clouds of glory, and part of this glory is an enthusiasm for simply *everything*. A three-year-old in his harassed mother's arms says 'Look! The dustbin lorry!' He has seen this fascinating object so few times that each time it arrives in his street, it draws from him a passionate cry of attention. A child lies in bed, and her father, having read the story, kisses her and goes to the light switch. 'Daddy – why do you always turn the darkness on?' Of course, to the accustomed vision, the father is turning the light off. But to the Martian, he might just as well be turning the darkness on. A three-year-old boy asks his mother, as she puts away his pram, 'Are you saving that for when I'm a baby again?' This is evidence of the cleaned perception that young children bring with them into the world.

Are we listening? What does that child know? He has come to us according to Wordsworth 'Not in entire forgetfulness / And not in utter nakedness'. Can we help children capture these perceptions before adolescence makes them self-conscious and more conventional in their perceptions? Wordsworth is passionate in his defence of the child's vision

('Ode: Intimations of Immortality from recollections of Early Childhood'). Picasso has similar insights. He says that he could draw like Raphael at eighteen, and had spent the rest of his life trying to draw like a child. If we are attentive to these ways of seeing things, we will hear little raw pieces of poetry in our children's mouths.

William Blake, Grigson tells us (1982: 152), 'once advised Samuel Palmer to stare at a knot in a piece of wood until it frightened him'. Children look harder at things than the rest of us, because their looking is fresher. This exercise, based on Craig Raine's poem, makes children look at everyday things very hard. It also makes them, indeed forces them, into using new metaphors, because they are not permitted to name the thing they are observing (the newly-arrived Martian doesn't seem to know the names of things, only what they are like). I have said before that poetry depends on 'defamiliarisation' – a process of making the familiar unfamiliar, if only for the moment. This technique helps that process. It is an extreme form of metaphor.

While working on a course for young writers, the poet Mick Gowar and I read Craig Raine's poem to some eleven-year-olds. We stood on a hill in Malvern, and looked around at everything, and tried to see each object as a Martian would. Later, back in the Youth Hostel where we were staying, Charlotte wrote this poem. It works much as Anglo-Saxon riddles work, of which more later:

A Martian goes for a walk

There are great big brains
tied to the ground and multi-coloured thoughts fly

around and rest on them.
Humans' giant pets get lost and roam around

the roads making strange noises.
as if they are in pain, yet no-one cares.

Strange things attached to humans carry
things around.

They put something in one end and when you
least expect it plop out it

comes again!

Massive giant heads are buried in the ground.
Most have squealing boxes attached.

If you break a giant's eye it makes the
most horrid sound.

There is some sort of animal that never
moves but humans are scared of it.

They feed it on paper that has an approval
stamp on.

Sometimes a daring human doctor
mends their stomach aches.

On great big spacecraft landing-fields humans
have two temples, one at each end. They have

these sometimes trapped in boxes with hundreds
of people, some kicking gifts at gods in the temples.

Giants sleep in the distance but their blanket
doesn't cover the whole body.

....
Charlotte, 11

Charlotte has looked at: trees with birds in, cars (I think), dogs, houses
with foundations, burglar alarms and windows (the eyes), postboxes,
letters with stamps on, postmen, football fields with goals and players
and, I think, the Malvern hills. Writing in this way has, first, made her
looking intense. I remember watching her eyes as she examined the landscape under the pressure of our inquisition: 'What else on earth that
you've seen does that remind you of, Martian? What is that like –
exactly?' And later: 'Can you think of a metaphor for that? Or a simile? A
very precise one?' The writing has had another advantage. It has made
her mix the registers of her language. She is able to refer to the hills in the
language of bedtime ('blanket'), football fields in terms of temples, and
postboxes in terms of medicine. This enriches her language as she writes,

but it also teaches her through direct experiences much about the potential for her language in the future. It also forces her away from the domain of the cliché.

This poem is by no means perfect, obviously. In places, it's raw and crude, much as Raine's poem must have been in its early life. Charlotte has looked at the shape of 'A Martian Sends . . .', which is composed of unrhymed couplets, and copied it, but her breaks – both between lines and stanzas – are not always appropriate in the way that Raine's are. She has used too many adjectives, and she repeats the word 'around' too often near the beginning. The word 'thing' is weak, and with thought, under sensitive questioning, she could have found a stronger one.

There is an understandable urge for the teacher to make things 'better' – for example, by changing:

> There is some sort of animal that never
> moves but humans are scared of it.
>
> They feed it on paper that has an approval
> stamp on.
>
> Sometimes a daring human doctor
> mends their stomach aches.
>
> On great big spacecraft landing-fields . . .

to:

> There is some sort of animal that never moves
> but humans are scared of it.
>
> They feed it on paper that has an approval stamp on.
> Sometimes a daring human doctor
>
> mends their stomach aches.
> On spacecraft landing-fields . . .

but note that if we fall to this temptation, we will have to decide what to do with the perfect line breaks in the section about the dog:

They put something in one end and when you
least expect it plop out it

comes again!

Now that Charlotte is in my past, and I in hers, such alteration would be a
pointless cosmetic finish on the face of her learning; much like pretty margins are on the edges of children's writing.

   Another group of children visited a church, and in a Martian poem otherwise less sparkling than Charlotte's, ten-year-old Lotte wrote four
powerful lines about the crucifixes:

There are men with curses on them
that hang from the wall on sticks
with melancholy expressions
on their poor, cursed faces.

....
Lotte, 10

As Shklovsky puts it: '. . . the essential function of poetic art is to counter-
act the process of habituation encouraged by routine everyday modes of
perception' (Hawkes 1977). In other words, poetic devices like rhyme,
assonance, alliteration, stanza form all serve to make the world strange, so
that we can look at the world again, and examine it, rather than merely see
it. As Hawkes (whose 1977 book quotes Shklovsky) says, we have become
'anaesthetised' to our environment, and the poetic function of *ostrananie*
(Shklovsky's Russian word meaning 'making strange') serves to make our
environment new again, so that we can get some kind of grip on it. So that
we can *feel* it. So that we can be Martians.

RIDDLES AND SNAPSHOTS

Another way of making things unfamiliar is through a poetic device akin
to the simile and the metaphor. This form has been debased in recent years
('What do you get if you dial 666? The Australian Police') but has been a
vital form for poetry down the centuries. Kevin Crossley-Holland has
translated the Exeter Riddle Book (1979) and many modern poets have
used the form, especially in verse written for children (see, for example,
John Cotton in Cotton and Sedgwick 1996: 41-3). Here is a riddle I wrote
after facing a class of children in a town I'd never visited before:

I have twenty-eight faces,
    fifty-six eyes.
Some parts of me are happy
    and some are full of sighs.

Parts of me are topped with gold,
    parts with brown
and I am a strange, many-coloured creature
    in a strange town.

I asked the children in another class to write a riddle in which the answer, as it were, was speaking. Here are some of their attempts:

I am a distinct colour
That has no colour.
I hold things together
On special days.
You have to work to find my end.
I am not praised for my many uses.
I start long
But am torn short
by sharp fangs.

                           (answer: sellotape)

....
Jack, 11

I whisper and wail
And whip and whirl
Covering the moon
With my helpful slaves
I scold the sun
Yet am fire's friend.
I am water's life,
Moving it under my touch.
You cannot see me,
Only watch me act.
I am God's breath.

                            (answer: wind)

....
Janine, 11

I am invisible ropes holding you down
pulling you down for safe keeping.
I want everything, and everything is mine.
Why do you want to escape?
You never will. Only few have succeeded
but they always return or die trying.
My friends are the sun, moon and stars.
I am the most selfish thing in the world.

(answer: gravity)

....
Alison, 10

Sometimes a riddle is beautiful but loose, and the answer disappoints:

I am a lion with freckles.
I am a lion with spots and the wind.
I have the waves curled around.

I have the land and the people.
I have the sea and the air.
I have the water from the taps.

I have the sun in the air.
I have the moon in the dark.
I have the clothes and the warmth.
. . .

(answer, rather anti-climactically, tiger)

....
Charlotte, 9

Another way of writing riddles is to play what Sandy Brownjohn (1982) calls 'The Furniture Game'. In the examples in Chapter 10, the answers to the 'I have' riddles are famous people. In the following example, an eleven-year-old girl has written about her sister:

Unji

She's an angry bull
and no matter how hard you try
you can't stop yourself
bringing out a red cloth.

She's a storm raging across the sea
and when she sighs
she sends a gale across the ocean.

She's a big room in a mansion.
It has many ornaments in it.
Although it sparkles
it hasn't been tended for a while.

She's a sour black coffee
made from cold tap water
which has sugar in it
but it's very hard to taste.

She's an overture in classical music.
She starts off quiet and tempting
but then ...
loud and fierce.

She is dreaming about when she passes her exams,
wearing the long black uniform.
She is also dreaming
about getting the job she wanted.

....
Renu, I I

In my introduction, I said that the range of concerns present in what is
called Personal, Social and Moral Education are always present in children's poems. In Renu's writing we can see a child reflecting on a loving
and tempestuous relationship with her sister. We can see this even more
clearly in the work on relatives in chapter 11, in the section on relationships

with the rest of the world. In all the work quoted in this chapter, we see children taking a chance to look at the world at a different angle from the usual one: 'Sometimes a daring human doctor / mends their stomach aches'; 'I whisper and wail / And whip and whirl / Covering the moon / With my helpful slaves'. 'She's an overture in classical music' . . . This enables learning both about the subject of the poems, and about the language they use.

A LITTLE LOOK: SNAPSHOT POEMS

The Martian exercise is about getting a different angle on things. About seeing things along a different aspect of our relationship with them. But so is all poetry, and our task as teachers is, among other things, to be alert to new possibilities. Edwin Morgan is a poet whose work is rich with such opportunities. In one poem he transcribes a conversation between a space traveller from Earth, and a Mercury dweller (1982: 259); in others there are words written by the first computers learning to communicate on their own (1982: 159, 268, 269). What interests me here are two techniques. In one poem, Morgan imagines an apple speaking (1982: 226). Children take very readily to this idea, and produce work that is stronger than they know:

Banana Song

'Grab me please, grab me, unpeel me quick
and let me take a dip
into your ghost cave.
I am warm in this skin,
I am thin as a pin,
and I want to take a dip
in your ghost cave, QUICK'.

....
Amanda, 11

No poet is justified in insisting that his or her meaning for a poem is the only possible one. Indeed, readers collude in the writing of a poem, because they bring to that poem (or novel or film, or play or whatever) a large amount of baggage, consisting of their life stories, memories of that life (these two are not the same thing, of course), things forgotten, things forgotten but about to be remembered because of the poem, things that have happened today and so on. We might see this baggage in other terms: our psychology, our spirituality, our politics. This is why poems that tell us too much – tell us, perhaps, what to feel, or think – fail. We feel frustrated unless we can bring to bear our own lives on a poem. This poem was, for Amanda, about what a banana might feel about being eaten: it is desperate to be eaten, the ghost cave is the mouth. But to us as adults, even if we read the poem casually, there are latent sexual meanings. This should keep us alert to the danger of patronising children as innocents.

Another way of writing that Edwin Morgan invented is the instamatic poem (1982: 203ff). Incidentally, the extraordinary variety of forms and subject matter make Morgan's work a fruitful field for a teacher interested in extending his or her children's writing. I wrote this one at the end of a school field one lunchtime. I must admit I cut away much extraneous material that at the time (to judge from my notebook) seemed vital:

> A woman in a garden flaps a sheet
> and turns to her baby scrambling
> free on the wonderful grass. An aeroplane
> wings overhead, like a fly on ice.

Children readily write instamatic poems. Look at the work of these ten-year-olds. I gave them subjects, and then one minute to write something down, or to take an instant picture of it. I suggested they might balance their poems round the word 'like' to provide a simile:

Two little Viking poems

The Vikings killed people
like a virus in a hospital. People screamed
like a bird screeching.

....
Kate, 10

The old Viking ship
sails in from sea
like a tired turtle
coming into lay its eggs.

....
Helen, 10

These poems used related images. Those eggs and that disease seemed unpleasantly, appropriately eloquent, and part of an image of evil growth that suits the subject, invasion and then alteration.

> The whale slaps its tail on the water
> like a boy clapping his hands.
>
> ....
> **Kate, 10**

This originally read 'like a child clapping their hands', and I talked to Kate for a few moments about the grammatical inconsistency of the singular noun 'child' and the plural pronoun 'their'. She came back to me with the sentence changed.

> The music is like fish going up one note to the surface of the sea.
>
> ....
> **Kayleigh, 10**

> Piano keys are like
> two dolphin jumping
> in and out of the
> water.
>
> ....
> **Adam, 10**

Both of these were written after I'd played a chord of C, note by note, on the piano. 'The music is like fish going up one note to the surface of the sea' strikes me as a perfect sentence, its monosyllabics neatly enacting a finger playing separate notes.

The whole exercise was riddled with the word 'like', which is, of course, central to the notion of simile. I have found that making the word central to our conversations about the world in the classroom enriches children's sentences in speech, and then, of course, their poems.

Chapter 6

'The dragging of dead thrushes'

Writing about nature

ANIMALS

Most children love animals, and those who don't are often frightened of them. This gap between love and fear suggests an obsession, or at least an intensity, a fascination. Adam in the garden had as a first task (before, apparently, Eve was made) to name the animals: '. . . the Lord formed every beast of the field, and every fowl of the air; and brought them unto Adam to see what he would call them . . .' Naming was obviously a primary act. Children name their pets: Twinkle, perhaps, or Scottie, or Eric, after a favourite singer or footballer. At a school I saw a little balsa wood cross under a tree, and fresh flowers beside it, and the word MOPSA in capitals written along the crosspiece.

This naming is one of the beginnings of poetry, one of the tributaries that flows into the main river. Arguably, it is the main stream. 'Imagination is the ability to name cats', writes Auden (after Samuel Butler, quoted in Brownjohn 1989). Poems like Edward Thomas's 'Adlestrop', 'Old Man' and 'Lob' (1936) show how important names are – in this case, the names of a quintessential Englishman:

> The man you saw, – Lob-lie-by-the-fire, Jack Cade,
> Jack Smith, Jack Moon, poor Jack of every trade,
> Young Jack, or old Jack, or Jack What-d'ye-call,
> Jack-in-the-hedge, or Robin-run-by-the-wall,
> Robin Hood, Ragged Robin, lazy Bob,
> One of the Lords of No Man's Land, good Lob, –
> Although he was seen dying at Waterloo,
> Hastings, Agincourt, and Sedgemoor too, –
> Lives yet . . .

Very young children develop a fascination for a particular animal: elephants, often, or whales, and their bedrooms become shrines to some breed. Children's literature recognises this: looking along my son's shelves, I find dogs, cats, lions, elephants, tigers and various unnameable wild things. Sometimes these animals are there for their own sake, and sometimes they stand for human characteristics. At best, arguably, they stand for a place in between. Perhaps as children, the human race is playing at being beginners again, practising following God and starting life. Children are closer to the earth. Like the creatures they love and fear, they are still obsessed with mud, and they burrow down to some essential truth.

One eight-year-old girl, Stephanie, was made like a wren. Brown-haired, tiny, dark-eyed, obsessively examining what was around her, she told me her six favourite words were: brown, dark, black, root, deep, bog. There is part of that troglodyte in all of us. In children, it is less likely to have been dreamed away as it is in adults. Children have at least the impulse to study, to know, to understand. Any ways we can offer them to understand animals will also help them to understand their language in all its intricacy. The language serves the animals, and the animals serve the language.

This nine-year-old boy writes:

Cat

I am the lolling, curled up in the chair
in the airing cupboard,
in trees,
on roofs, in drawers,
behind closed curtains.

I am the dragging of dead thrushes
across the garden.
I am the raider of nests,
the fighter.
I am the flurry of teeth and claws,
the grabber of fingers.

I am the creeping down low,
the dead straight look,
zip,
the pounce.

I am the purr on someone's lap,
the big wail in a fight.

I am the king of wailing that makes
people throw boots at me.
I am the green headlights
piercing the dark.

I am the stalking along the path,
the pushing of doors open
with my nose,

the doing of things you don't want me do to,
the not doing of things you want me to do.

....
Daniel, 9

I have written before in this book (citing Leonardo da Vinci) about how we need prisons to free ourselves to write. Here is another cell. This writer observes a cat immaculately ('the pushing of doors open/with my nose' for example, and 'the green headlights/piercing the dark') under a constraint that has forced him to describe the cat entirely in terms of its actions. He is writing (in other words) in present participles. He thus manages phrases that can stand for the whole animal, if only for a moment (what else is a present participle if not the capturing of a moment?). This poem is an example of close observation of a mental image made unfamiliar by a grammatical condition. It drives the writer, at the end, into an unwitting (presumably) echo of St Paul: '. . . for what I would, that do I not; but what I hate, that do I' (Romans 7:15).

When we are writing about the external world, nothing is more potent than first-hand experience. This is a valuable truism (if not a platitude). Perhaps it's a cliché! And in terms of my comments in my interlude I ought to have cut what, obviously, I haven't. The problem here is that clichés, platitudes and truisms are usually, by their nature, true. In using them, we are, at best, taking on the received wisdom of our predecessors. This shouldn't discourage us from trying to do better. In any case, my cliché is only a cliché for some of us. Others (some politicians, for example) might well prefer children to learn from second-hand materials: textbook articles about birds, for example, or CD ROM articles, or the Lambs' *Tales from Shakespeare*, rather than birds themselves, in flight, at rest, nesting, or the plays of Shakespeare himself. He probably doesn't think of 'first-hand experience' as 'potent' at all.

The next examples are of close observation of an animal which is physically present. I quoted earlier Tardios' remark (Pirrie 1986) that the world is 'troubled/with a lack of looking'. Observe this boy looking at a trout on a plate in his classroom. There is some Martian writing here, I think. The cheese grater and the silver pineapple are perfect metaphors made by someone who has seen, on the one hand, a trout, for the first time, or, on the other, a cheese grater and a silver pineapple.

Trout

Its skin is wet and firm.
It's a cheese grater
or a silver pineapple,
its mouth a dark cave
armed with razor teeth.

Its fleshy belly
without scales
hangs lifelessly down.

Its face is stunned. Look:
its home team have just gone down 1-0
to a rubbish team.
It's seen a bad car crash.
It's seen a friend get into a fight.
It's been given an expensive present.

Its gills are silent breathers
designing air out of water.

Its fins act as a rudder.

It is a bullet
shining in and out of rocks.

....
John, 9

Actually, the last lines read, as this boy wrote them up:

His gills are silent breathers
designing air out of water.

His fins act as a rudder.

He is a bullet
shining in and out of rocks.

Why did I suggest that he change this? First, because I didn't want the
inept change (as I saw it) from 'it' to 'him'. Second, possibly, I was thinking
as I typed 'him': 'Why should the creature be a him?' But now I'd like to
admire, and ask about, the learning, which is far more important than such
essentially cosmetic changes. Notice first how this writer doesn't rest with
one metaphor. First there's the cheese grater and then the silver pineapple,
as if he knows that one of these images may eventually fall during a possible drafting process: not precise enough. Notice, too, how the writer is
prepared to take risks. That is another Martian characteristic. The lines:

its home team have just gone down 1-0
to a rubbish team.
It's seen a bad car crash.

are a good distance over the top, but no writer unprepared to risk the
extreme will ever approach the edges of what both observation and language can achieve. It is because of the willingness to take this kind of risk
that this writer can manage lines like:

His gills are silent breathers
designing air out of water.

This child is also learning that nothing is too small for the attention of
poetry. Observation of a spider's web, say – or the juddering engine of a
car, or the way a shadow moves along a brick wall as the day progresses –
all these can lead to epiphanies, moments of understanding and delight, as
observation of this trout has.
   For writers (and all artists) seeing is nothing without the power of making
your readers see what you see. That isn't true, of course, if you merely want
to walk on the cliffs and look down at the waves, or merely watch the wind
distort the corn, or merely study the plumage on an exotic bird at the zoo. I
repeat the word 'merely' there deliberately, of course, because to do these
things isn't to do something small, but to relish a part of our humanity. But

the artist has to take a step further, and make the reader see what s/he has seen. Much false poetry is written without the reader being taken into account. It may be therapeutic, but it isn't poetry.

The following poem is written in pencil on A4 paper arranged landscape-fashion. First, the child has drawn a butterfly: it's a large brown creature with eye patterns on its wings and a purple stripe. It has a beaming smile on its face. The poem is arranged all around this picture, and the lines are exactly as I have given them here:

The butterfly

The butterfly feels
like a velvet curtain
flapping in the wind.
a feast of cobwebs
a green leaf.
a scrap of fur.
It sounds like
the wind whispering
the pitter patter little feet
it's like
scraps of paper
blowing in the wind
a thought
dancing in my head
a leaf floating
from the trees.

....
Ceryl, 6

I do not understand all this imagery: the velvet curtain, for example, isn't entirely clear to me, though I know what Ceryl is driving at. But some of the metaphors are perfect: 'scraps of paper/blowing in the wind/a thought/dancing in my head'.

How has Ceryl arrived at this conclusion? First, I would suggest it was important that she drew the butterfly first. Often this apparently very different activity enables the writer to subconsciously search for words as she draws. I am always struck by the way children go calm as they draw – assuming, of course, that the activity they have been offered is one of high quality. Behind this calmness is a buzz of internal intellectual word activity that can produce writing like this. Behind this, in other words, are thoughts dancing in the head.

What is Ceryl learning about? First, she is reinforcing her attentive admiration for butterflies, as she thinks purposefully about them; she is increasing her self-esteem as a private interest becomes a legitimate subject for school activity; she is learning what her language can do; and she is learning more about butterflies by a kind of poised attention to them that the drawing and writing together have brought about. And as far as we as teachers are concerned, we have to relearn day-by-day how much we can gain from a proper attention to children's work.

The four-year-olds in a nursery school in the next example are composing poems about animals. 'Composing' is the important word here, because they didn't write them down. The teacher asked the children to tell her about animals that they cared about, and she wrote down their words. She then read the material back to the children, and asked them which words were important enough to repeat.

Pigs

> A long time ago we went to a farm.
> We were on holiday and it was raining.
> The pigs were lying down on their house.
> They were getting soaking wet.
>
> A long time ago we went to a farm.
> I think the pigs were wild pigs.
> I was really quiet.
> I went right up to one of the pigs
> And touched his back.
>
> A long time ago we went to a farm.
> The pig's back felt hairy and rough.
> The pig made a snuffly, pig noise.
> His back felt rough, like wire.
>
> A long time ago we went to a farm.
> The pigs had squashy faces.
> They were lying about in mud.
> They were smelly, like a bin.
>
> ....
> **Anna, 4**

I have written about children and the deaths of animals in chapter 8, but one example, another cat, fits here:

My Cat

My cat is at the vet's
and she's not coming back.
She used to scratch me.
She used to go in the garden
to go to the toilet everyday.

My cat is at the vet's
and she's not coming back.
Her name was Polly.
She was brown and white
with tiny scratchy claws

My cat is at the vet's
and she's not coming back.
She got sick.
She was sick on the landing.
Mummy had to clean it up.

My cat is at the vet's
and she's not coming back.
Polly had to go to the vet's
and come home lots of times.
The vet said he couldn't do anything for Polly.

My cat is at the vet's
and she's not coming back.
Now I keep asking Mummy
for a rabbit
but she won't let me.

....
Charlotte, 4

Let's look closely at some of the phrases used here. 'I went right up to one of the pigs and touched his back' tells us about the nervous excitement the child felt at doing something unfamiliar and even, possibly, dangerous. It also reminds the child of that experience as she speaks the words. The words are evidence of her learning about pigs, of course; about language; but also about her own courage. 'Rough, like wire' is a simile that is both tactile and pictorially vivid at the same time. In the second poem, the repeated phrase 'and she's not coming back' is a telling and sad under-statement, evidence of how children listen to their parents' words even when they don't seem to be doing so. I think these poems are evidence of the fact that not only are very young children poets; they are also capable of fresh metaphor and phrasing, of putting familiar cadences in unfamiliar settings to move us, and remind us of times when the pet animal went to the vet's and didn't come back. More important, 'My Cat' is a respectful catalogue of a child's memories, of her courage and pain. It is a funeral ora-tion for Polly.

The Cat

Answers are everywhere.

Salman Rushdie was quoted recently as saying that everybody has answers, but it is the writer's job to ask questions. I am struck listening to politicians that interviewers' *questions* are almost always more informative and articulate that the politicians' *answers*. The questions articulate what we want to know, what troubles us, whether they are about the eating of beef, or about cease-fires. But the answers uniformly blow smoke. Questions were central to the following work. I give below my words to a class of ten-year-olds, and a commentary on those words. This is followed by extracts from their writing:

> There is a cat in your head, not just any old cat, a particular one, perhaps your own cat, or your neighbours' . . . Look at its face. What shapes can you see there? In the eyes? The mouth? What colours? As it opens its mouth, what does the roof of the mouth remind you of? Watch the cat move away. Can you think of some words that describe that move-ment? What does the cat's fur feel like or remind you of when it moves against your leg? . . .

I leave huge silences between the questions. Schools, which are places where human beings are sent in order to learn to think about everything, rarely give those humans any time for serious thought. Just think of all the elements in school life that work against reflection: the noise, of course, but also the sheer number of human beings crammed into one place; and the multiplicity of tasks to be done, and the administrative nature of many of those . . . the huge silences between my questions here may not offer much, but there is the possibility for a little reflection in them. And the quality of what the children say is improved by them, because in the silence they have the opportunity to use words, to frame them, to work with the ineffable relationship of word to thought.

> Cat with angry look
> with back arching like a
> rainbow without colours.

....
Corinne, 10

> Head is a
> stuffed head
> with marbled eyes,
> and velvet nose foam.

....
Mike, 10

> When the tongue comes out it is curved like a cup.
> The milk gets caught on the bumps of the tongue
> and gets lifted into the cat's mouth . . .

....
Michael, 10

> It stretches its front legs out
> and brings them back slowly.
> Then like a dash of lightning he pounces . . .

....
Nicola, 10

The demands of poetry – with its insistence that things should be both right and new – are huge demands on our capacity for reflection, for contemplation, for the study of a trout, say, that makes it look, for the moment, like a cheese grater, or a silver pineapple. Because of that fact, time spent on poetry is repaid in all other areas of the curriculum where we need to think. All thought about anything for the purpose of writing about it will be changed one day into light across our path.

WATER: THE SWIMMING POOL

The six-year-olds in the next example were writing with me immediately before a swimming lesson at the local baths.

> You can see steam coming off the water. It looks like smoke . . . It smells like the toilet stink and it smells like an elephant house . . . When you shout it bounces off the wall like you've said it again . . . The swimming pool smells like a frog has thrown up . . . The water feels slimy up my nose . . . The water stings like gentle insect legs in my eyes . . . It is frightening with my head under the water, like I'm going to die . . .

After the swimming lesson, the teacher collected more phrases:

> My legs go wobbly and my hair sticks to my face . . . You feel sticky and tired . . . My arms and legs are tired and I can't stop thinking about lunch . . .

Again, this work demonstrated the power of children's thinking when they are pushed in the silence to think and feel. Though some of the phrases are sloppy and conventional (for example, 'smells like the toilet stink') that is the price we have to pay as teachers for the moments, usually coming later, when the children surprise us: 'The water stings like gentle insect legs in my eyes'.

TO THE SUN

One immediate way to make writing about natural objects more vigorous is to ask children not to write *about* them at all, but *to* them, as the pharaoh Akhenaten did with the sun. This pharaoh is credited by many for reforming the multi-god religion of Egypt into a monotheistic one focused on aspects of the sun's life-giving qualities, for establishing a tradition of relatively naturalistic art in which, for example, the royal family's daily life was depicted, and for freedom of expression in art. Here is part of his great hymn to the sun, in a version by Emily Roeves:

You created the sun
when you were far away –
men, cattle, all flocks –

everything on the earth moving with legs,
creeping, stalking, striding,
flying, or gliding above with wings.
Foreign countries
and the land of Egypt:
you placed every man in his place
and you provide his food.

You are the Creator of Months,
the Maker of Days.
You are the Counter of Hours!

You shine on the eastern horizon
and fill the whole earth with your beauty
and while you are far away
your beams shine in every face.

When you shine
creatures live.
When you set
they die.
You yourself
are lifetime.
In you do creatures live.

Living disc,
Lord of all that was created
and which exists –
your beams have brightened
the whole earth.

The slightly wordy, anything-goes feel of this helps to set children free. Catching the tone nearly perfectly, Amanda wrote:

You light up the sky like a sapphire.
You are the moon's enemy.
One day you will be destroyed
Sun.
You glow so bright that sometimes
I can't even see what's in front of me.

But just by your light
you can beat the moon and then you will not be destroyed sun.
You help us live. Without you there would be nothing around.

You're our life sun, so don't let yourself be destroyed
Sun.
Then you will have a celebration with the clouds.

....
Amanda, 8

We can see what Amanda is aiming at: the repetition of 'Sun' (twice iso-
lated on a line) emphasises that this is an address *to* the sun, rather than a
more commonplace poem *about* the sun. We can see her similes flourish,
and we can admire her metaphorical gusto.

In the next example (from Sedgwick 1989), ten-year-olds are using the
technique of metaphors to write about a foggy day:

The fog is as thick as a sheepskin.
Sometimes it looks like smashed glass,
like milk spinning.

....
Danielle, 10

When it comes
cobwebs are just white hair
with hair spray on.
It's a mirror
all smoked up ...

....
Sarah, 10

...Tiny clouds gather for meetings ...
But some foglings come
and gather trouble ...

....
Sarah, 10

'Thick as a sheepskin . . . smashed glass . . . milk spinning . . . white hair with hair spray on . . . a mirror all smoked up . . . ' These are no more and no less than children practising their craft as writers.

A kenning (I have quoted Brownjohn in correspondence elsewhere [1994b])

> was an Old Norse technique used in writing or storytelling which was a new descriptive name, usually two words, based on an attribute of the original; for example, 'swan's way' for the sea, or 'Beo-wulf' – the enemy (wolf) of the bee, i.e. a bear . . .

Similarly, *Medved* is the Serbo-Croat for bear: *med* = honey, *ved* = eat. We can use kennings to write about anything:

Winter kenning

Nose-redeemer
ear-nipper
white bird drifting
crunchy carpet
hider, concealer
freezing ammunition
white person with carrot and pipe
the sledge's path
sudden water pouring away
winter memory.

LIES

Throughout this book there is a tension between strict form and self-expression – as there must be in any book about teaching poetry (and about teaching any other art, come to that). As Coleridge knew, poetry shows up 'a more than usual state of emotion with more than usual order' (quoted in Hourd 1949: 87). Notice that, in contrast with some writers I have quoted so far, Coleridge doesn't insist we teach entirely through order; we need more feeling as well. But the feeling on its own, without form, is void: it merely helps children to produce writing that is slopping about in inefficient autobiography, a very tedious exercise.

The truest poetry (Touchstone memorably tells us in *As You Like It*) is the most feigning. One way of both feigning and approaching truth simultaneously is to tell lies (see Corbett and Moses 1986: 46). Of course, we can make a moral point here, a little hypocritically, perhaps, for which of us could get through a normal month without a few lies ('the cheque is in the post; 'that dress looks lovely'; 'that was delicious but I had a very big lunch')? We can quote the commandment that tells us we mustn't bear false witness, and talk about the effect that lying about our emotions has on our lives.

But Picasso says that art is a lie told to tell the truth, and there are many ways in which this is true. First, if we tell the obvious truth – the physical one that most of us can verify without any emotional or intellectual effort – we are boring. 'The tree trunk is brown' . . . 'The grass is green'. 'After days of darkness, the sun has at last come out.' What we need here is a way of extending these truths, and I hope that this book is full of such ways. Not that these 'obvious truths' are always true: Carl Rogers points out that very few tree trunks are brown. Lavender and mouse grey, yes (Rogers 1970).

Second, the act of distortion is a creative act in itself. I remember a head-teacher I worked with who used to tell funny stories about school journeys. 'I told him this . . . and then I found him doing that . . . and he said . . .' One day his wife overheard him telling me one of these stories, and she said, 'But that didn't happen to you, Leslie, it happened to Norman, the head at Hill Farm, and he told you about it'. And Leslie replied, 'I know, but it makes it more interesting telling the stories this way'. Deplorable as his behaviour was, it makes a point for me: we create and recreate as we live. Or we can. This exercise owns up to the power of fiction, of distortion.

Lies about the sun

1   The sun needs a pair of duracel batteries twice every week.
2   It is a tiny ball of ice, painted with bright yellow paint from our school.
3   Deep in the night when the sun disappears he nips down to Pallion to Betty's fish shop to buy a pattie lot.
4   I used to keep the sun in my back garden until the green party told me that I had to set it free.
5   The sun used to be my uncle Henry but one day the queen's magician turned him into a big yellow balloon and gave it to me, but I lost my grip and it flew into the sky. And there he stays.
6   There isn't really a sun. Only people who desperately need glasses can see the sun.

....
Victoria, 10

In that example, the licence to lie has set Victoria free to expose wit, verbal ebullience and a remarkable sense of rhythm. Her easy use of local refer-ence ('Pallion . . . Betty's fish shop . . . pattie lot') sharpens the focus of her work. In the next example, Jean's lies about a rainbow (which extend even to the title) lead to a tender, surreal lyricism:

The Stormbow

As I look at you oh stormbow
With your dull as ditchwater browns

With the red indigo at the bottom leading up to
The indigo in the highest heights

I long to sit in your dish
The semi-circular hole as your ends reach up to the sky

Once when the world began
I climbed your sides

I reached the top and met
A bird in the clouds

One day I'll climb you again
Stormbow in the sky

....
Jean, 11

A certain poignancy is provoked here by a lying creativity. Or should that be the other way around? If I might return to the human body for a moment, eleven-year-old Saesha wrote an astonishing lie poem about her eye. I printed it in my book (1994b) in an uncorrected version. This is how the poem ended up, after consultation with an editing friend and the child's teacher:

Ten Lies about my Eyes

My eye can turn right round
and I can see my brain
and in my brain there are lots of little people working
but in the night
when I turn my eyes around
the people are sleeping
on bunk beds

Sometimes
when I have no-one to play with at school
I take my eyes out
and bounce them up and down
and when girls come passing by
they scream and shout
Miss! She's taken her eyeball out!
So I quickly stuff it back in

and when I'm bored at home
of watching cartoons
I take my eye out
and throw it out the window
and it goes around the world
and I see that in other places of the world
it is much more exciting
because there are aliens
trying to take over the world

and when I feel it
it feels like a very flat piece of paper
so I just get a pencil and write a poem
and I call it
Ten lies about my eyes.

....
Saesha, 11

Rules are important to writers in part because they must break them. It is liberating to understand the mastery of a rule, and then to subvert it. This poem achieves much by breaking the conventions of normal narrative possibility, and each subversion leads to another, often larger one. Saesha has understood something a novelist said recently. When he started his first novel, he wrote the opening sentence down. Then he looked at it for a long time, realising slowly that now anything – *anything* might happen. By telling lies, Saesha manages to reflect on, and make public, her anxieties about loneliness and boredom. She writes with dangerous verve, and manages images that remind me, again, of surrealist painting: 'I can see my brain/ and in my brain there are lots of little people working . . . I take my eyes out/ and bounce them up and down . . .' She understands the power a writer has: she can make anything happen. She can change the world.

LIGHT

I have discussed simile and metaphor in chapter 2, pointing out that hands are useful resources for these figures of speech. Another useful resource is light, which was the scientific topic some eight-year-olds were studying, when Alison wrote:

The light is like
The shape of a baby's mobile
like the yellow in an advert

The light was like
a golden eagle climbing on the window
a zigzag around my bedroom.

Later on the light will be
a prince in sparkling love
but the love will fade away until another day

....
Alison, 8

A ten-year-old wrote:

The light was like a flash
from a place never heard of.

The light was like a path
flowing through the window pane.

The black cloud stands there
with rays of sun hanging, filling
our faces with joy.

The light is like an abstract of
different dark colours
all passing my mind.

....
Zubaida, 10

Extracts from other children's writing with this stimulus were:

[Sunset] The light will be like a rippled up orange swaying up down left and right the reflection spreading through the lake (Cara, 11).

The light was like a shimmering ruby setting itself in the night sky ... Now the light is like a white silk cloth blowing in the wind (Natasha, 9).

The light was like / a flickering flame caught in a prison of glass (Ben, 11).

All these examples show a vigorous use of language stemming from the word 'like' and further intensive questioning. Cara melds 'ripped' with 'rippled' to useful effect. This shows that confusion is not always bad news; that, indeed, it can have a lucky effect. The rest of her orange image is startling. It has the indispensable condition of surprise.

Some of these images might seem conventional, others far-fetched. But these children are practising; as, indeed, are these next children, who have been feeling fruit, vegetables and bread just before a harvest festival. The teacher had asked them what they liked about these objects. That was easy to answer: smoothness, softness, hardness. But by the simple urgency of always pushing forward, she managed to get the children to extend their thinking and their learning – and, of course, their writing.
  'I like the feel of the bread', six-year-old Jennifer told the class, 'because it is bumpy.' The teacher looked straight at Jennifer and said, 'Bumpy as what?' There was a longish silence here. As teachers we tend to fill in these silences because they are embarrassing in normal social intercourse, and because they may be distressing to the child. But what learning happens entirely without distress? And, as it turned out, the rewards for Jennifer were great. After a long think, she said, 'Bumpy as a bouncy castle'. This isn't particularly strong, but the first reward was in the fact that Jennifer now understood a principle: that you can compare unlike things that do have a sudden temporary likeness (like the trout and the cheese grater I've quoted earlier). She went away and wrote the first draft. After some discussion, she rearranged her writing like this:

I like the feel of the bread
because it is bumpy as a bouncy castle.
I like the smell of the bread
because it smells like buttered sweetcorn.
I hate the smell of the onion

because it smells like chopsticks.
I like the feel of the onion
because it is all crumbly like a butterfly's wings when they've just come out
of a chrysalis.

....
Jennifer, 6

Notice how this grows from the hit and miss of all the lines up to 'chop-sticks'; then Jennifer's reward (and ours as readers) is the lovely comparison of the skin of an onion with the butterfly's wings. In this last line we can see that two-way learning. Who can say whether, as she writes this, the image of the onion, or the image of the butterfly's wings were the more prominent in her mind? Either way, we have to be deaf not to hear, or at least sense, the learning. Notice, too, how the writer intensifies this image with the last, precise eight words. These are words so demanding that they slide across the line structure the writer had thought out for herself. Jennifer was now beaming around the room, delighted with her work – which had taken her nearly an hour's thought and writing.

VISITS

While I emphasise that almost all successful work in writing poetry grows from first-hand experiences, this does not necessarily mean that the subject of the poem has to be physically present for the poem to work. Even if the cat or the sister or the bicycle is not present in the room as the child writes, the teacher can, by asking pointed questions, bring it into the child's head. What Hamlet calls 'the mind's eye' is a powerful visual tool, as I hope I've shown. But to present children with tangible objects in the classroom or, even better, to take them out of school, is to do many things that are educational. It is to de-school the world if only for the time being. It is to present the children with their environment as it is, in its ugliness and its beauty, unfiltered for the moment through our teachers' middle-class spectacles.

I went to Grizedale Forest Park with children from Whalley Primary School, their headteacher, Gordon Askew, teachers, parents and governors. The Park is (in the words of Bill Grant in Grant and Harris 1991) 'a magical forest, tucked away in the fells of Furness in the southern Lake District'. Since 1977 it has been dotted with sculptures, some toning in with the environment, others contrasting with it, but still complementing it. Examples of the first kind are *Forest Fugue* by David Kemp, which is composed of slates and trucks arranged to look like an organ playing, 'a silent requiem for the stumps' (Kemp); and the same artist's *Ancient Forester*, which is a huge man made entirely out of a single oak tree. He is leaning on a massive axe. An example of the second kind is *Ting* by Colin Rose, a forty foot diameter steel circle 'tightly woven through the branches of a tree' as Rose puts it. Other works include a magnificent giant rabbit by Alan Greenwood, and *Wild Boar Clearing* by Sally Matthews. These creatures are made out of mud and cement and (says Matthews) 'they will not last for many years. They will decay like their surroundings'.

It rained all morning when we were there, and we worried whether the day's work and pleasure would be washed away, but the day cleared just enough for us to walk around the forest. A nine-year-old wrote this poem next day in school, after having made drawings and notes on site:

The Ancient Forester Speaks

My horns are springy
like telephone wire.
I am too old and wrinkled
to cut down trees anymore.
Lines, carved and curled,
rot into my decaying skin . . .

....
Matthew, 9

One child wrote her poem in the old format best known in 'There was an old woman who swallowed a fly':

We went to Grizedale Forest

We went to Grizedale Forest
And the heavens opened.

We went to Grizedale Forest
And the heavens opened.
The hills rolled.

We went to Grizedale Forest
And the heavens opened.

The hills rolled
And the trees stood proud and tall.

We went to Grizedale Forest
And the heavens opened.
The hills rolled.
And the trees stood proud and tall.
The Ancient Forester guarded the path.

We went to Grizedale Forest
And the heavens opened.
The hills rolled.
And the trees stood proud and tall.
The Ancient Forester guarded the path
And night crawled over the forest.

....
Eleanor, 10

Ting provoked this poem from another nine-year-old:

Ting

The circle flings
and swings
like angels' wings.
The circle is a king
with precious things.
The circle swings
and flings.

....
Liam, 9

In this poem, the rhyme requirement that Liam has imposed on himself has led to a playfulness that is part of his personality. The first requirement of a poet (or any serious writer) is a love of language expressed in a need to play with it.

TRAVEL

In the next example, five six-year-old children are talking to their teacher about their holidays. It will be seen that the teacher has built the structure of the poem, but the words are all the children's. She says to each of the group in turn: 'Where did you go on holiday? How did you get there? What did you eat on the way? . . .' And later, when she has written their replies down, she asks them 'What did you do when you got there?' She pointed out to me how some of the replies were dull, especially at the beginning; but details brought the whole piece into focus. Also, all the children were very proud of their writing when it was read out loud, to much applause, to the teachers and the class later.

The Travel Poem

I went on the Isle of Wight
and on the boat
I had – I can't remember.

I went on a holiday
and in the car
I had – a rest.

I went on a train
to see Aunty Alison
and I had – nothing to eat.

I went on an aeroplane
to Disneyland
and I had – fish nuggets and chips.

I went on an aeroplane, as well,
to Spain
and we weren't allowed in the boats
because there were naughty fishes.

And on the Isle of Wight
Robin jumped on the other cliff
and my mum thought we had lost him

and when I got out of the car
I went on a bed settee
and watched TV

and at Aunty Alison's
I saw Stephanie Peach O'Neill
and she played with me, and loved me

and at Disneyland
I went on a roller coaster
and it flew up 'cos it went so fast

and in Spain
I looked at the pool
but I never went in
because of the naughty fishes.

These children are learning more with this work about something they understand much of already. That is the power of names to move and console and to bring back to our minds and hearts treasured times and relationships. They are also appreciating how much more important than they thought are their words and ideas – look, here is an adult writing them down! The words give me as a reader memorable glimpses into other families' lives: the moment when a child was lost, for example, and Stephanie Peach O'Neill, and the mysterious naughty fishes.

THE IMPORTANCE OF PLAYING WITH WORDS.

The main requirement for a committed writer is not an urge to entertain. Still less is it a need to make money. It is only in part (admittedly in large part) a need to search for the truth. Crucially, a writer must have a compulsion to play with words. The relationship between the child–writer and the rest of the world consists in significant part in language, and as s/he explores that relationship s/he learns about language. This book is full of examples of the pleasure to be had in such language games. One recent example is 'The circle flings/and swings/like angels' wings'. The game that provoked the following poem grew under a constraint that I did not, at the time, welcome. 'Our topic', a teacher told me, 'is dinosaurs. Can you get the children to write about that?' I was troubled by this, and I still am. How could I help the children play a word game while honouring the teacher's request?

My forest

My forest is where the lakes run fast.
The forest has a strong smell of fire from volcanoes.
The T Rex's skin is very soft and smooth.
The teeth are like long knives and it smells like dead flowers.
The plant-eating dinosaur has a neck like a long lamp-post.
Its tummy is like a big balloon that has got bigger.
The flying dinosaur's wings are like material.
It glides like a paper aeroplane.
I look up at the sky and see the dinosaurs
going in and out of clouds.

I asked the children to close their eyes and to cover them with their hands.
They imagined an ancient forest. It is easy to infer from the poem the questions I asked:

> You are in a forest in the age of the dinosaurs . . . What is going on? . . .
> What can you smell? . . . Here is a dinosaur? What does the creature's
> skin feel like? . . . Can you think of a metaphor for any part of its
> body . . .?

And so on. In this sort of play, writers inch towards a truth. Nothing so
simple as a truth of a scientific kind about dinosaurs, necessarily, but a
truth about their feelings about dinosaurs, and the relations between themselves and their language.

A note on writing about the human-made environment

W H Auden believed engines were beautiful things. In Carpenter (1981), there is a photograph of the poet at six years old with arms draped over a metal railing, eyes gazing down into the Rhayader water-works. The fact that the machines never answered back, but merely let the small boy adore them, was a huge point in their favour for the mature poet. His generation of poets famously celebrated railways, pylons and buildings. The stillness and strength of efficient machinery has a charm and power for most young children.

The bicycle

It sounds like
    a bee buzzing
    a snake hissing
    a rattlesnake hissing its tail
    a motor car
    a woodpecker pecking a tree
    a horse trotting
    the pitter-patter of a mouse
    raindrops rattling on the windows

The round wheel is spiky
It looks like
    a spinning wheel
    the sun is shining
    a bang!
    the windows of a little wooden house
    an eye with a pupil in the middle

When it's spinning it looks like a drill
   a bit of machine
whirling around
   an eye going around

The spokes look like they are not there

They are invisible
   They disappear
They vanish

The chain looks
   like the things bees keep honey in
– a honeycomb!

This poem was composed by a class of five-year-olds. I was working with the children, and the class teacher agreed to be the secretary, and write down what was composed. The order is mine, because of the sequence of questions, and the shape is the teacher's. But crucially, the children agreed to be the writers, the composers. The bicycle was upside down on a low table. This is important, because this de-familiarises the thing. Because children are used to seeing bicycles the right way up, they take aspects of them for granted.

I sat down on the carpet with the children, representing myself (not entirely untruthfully) as a learner alongside them. I asked them to hypothesise; What will happen if . . .? Then at last, I spun the wheel of the bicycle and asked the class to listen. What was the noise like? At first they imitated it with their lips, tongue and teeth, making a hissing noise, but I asked them for words. What does the noise remind you of? Once a child had produced a phrase of some clarity (the 'bee buzzing'), the others followed suit. I told them that all the phrases had to be different from each other.

Then I asked them for descriptions of what the bike looked like, first when the wheel was still, and then when it was spinning. It is important that, when they say a phrase that I don't understand, we leave it there. Their vision is likely to be fresher than mine, and to reject something just because I am a little jaded would give a wrong message. Later we reinforced the learning by asking the children to draw the bicycle, still upside down on the table.

An older group of children had a similar experience with my car engine. One of them wrote:

An elephant's trunk withdraws from an ice bucket.
The elephant's very gritty.
Four grass snakes crawl into a cardboard box.
When he revved the car up the snakes very nearly knocked the box over.

When the engine was turned on the snakes were frightened.
They were shaking.
There was a dead snake at the back.
His head had been burned off.

....
Graham, 11

Children can take a fresh look at the world, natural and mechanical, in many ways. A Martian stare, a riddling glance, creative lying that helps us to tell the truth, various kinds of naming . . . All this helps them to widen their vision from their fascinated look at themselves. What they do next is to link themselves to the rest of the world. What are the lines like that travel from their eyes, their minds, their hearts to the world outside them? In the next part of this book, I look at the meeting point between children's subjectivity, and the objects they confront.

Part III

Chapter 7

Introduction

Me and the rest of the world

I have written elsewhere (1994b) that

> [Personal, Social and Moral Education] is the whole curriculum – after all, what is there except me and the rest of the world? Every scientific and technological project, every painting, every dance, every musical performance is a research project into the relationship between me and the rest of the world . . .

I meant to write 'every poem' as well, but I guess now that it was too obvious in the context. Anyway, 'Me and the rest of the world' was mis-understood by a publisher to imply a dim egocentricity that was the opposite of what I meant. I am not, as pre-Copernican Man thought he was, the centre of things. I fully understand that the rest of the world – indeed, the rest of the universe – does not circle around me. Unless I under-stand that, I am not fit to be a social being, and nor is that publisher, and nor are the children we teach, or the readers for whom he produces books. By 'Me and the rest of the world' I meant that the world is there, and I am in it: how do I learn to take my part? Or, more particularly, given that this book is about classrooms, how do we teach children to live justly and cre-atively in that world?

We are connected to each other, and to all the components of the world we know. Famously, John Donne has already said this, with an earthier and infinitely stronger metaphor than the one I'm about to use, in his 17th Meditation:

> No man is an *Island*, entire of itself; every man is a piece of the *Continent*, a part of the *main* . . . if a clod be washed away by the sea, *Europe* is the less . . ., as well as if a *promontory* were . . .
> (*The Oxford Dictionary of Quotations* [1979: 190], his emphases)

My metaphor is geometrical: we have relationships that I think of as lines. Charges flow back and forth along those lines, some of which are short and strong. Others are stretched – but never to breaking point. They make up our complicated intellectual and imaginative relationship with the world. The arts help us to realise (in the pristine sense of the word, to *make real*) these relationships. In drawing, for example, we are familiar with the way children learn about relationships with objects as they look carefully, and attempt to record their angle on what they see (see Sedgwick and Sedgwick 1993). The lines here form a triangle, eye to object observed to pencil. In drama we can see children dealing with violent relationships as they learn about how to deal with bullying and bullies (Sedgwick 1994b: 83–8). In painting, we can see children coming to a provisional under-standing of pre-history and history, or music, like *The Blue Danube*, or African drums (see Sedgwick and Sedgwick 1996a).

This realisation, this making real, is even more true of writing poems than it is of the other arts, as Donne knew. A child simply can't write in the serious, reflective way we call poetry unless s/he has studied in mind and heart the distance, small or large, between his or her life, and the thing, or living being, outside him or her, that, for the moment, is an obsession; that obsesses in that uniquely creative way we see as the inspiration for a poem. In other words, as a writer, I have to see myself and the things (or living beings) observed as meaningless on their own, and only taking on mean-ing in terms of the relationships between them, and me. The real business of learning, of understanding, takes place not in me or the thing (or living being) but in the line I draw between myself and it with my writing. And that applies just as readily to children and their writing. 'I want to hear a baby tree/ breaking out of his seed,/ but I can't hear it', writes a child later in this part, desperately sketching that almost invisible line.

I think you can usefully reverse that equation. Unless you have written (or drawn, or danced, or made music, or acted), you can't study in your mind and heart the distances between. For artists, lines being taken for a walk are lines into knowledge. The line that pulls the sentences together has a similarly serious purpose. It is there to make relationships explicit, public, clear: relationships between us and what we are writing about, and the relationships between us and our language; and the relationship between the things we are looking at and the language they demand.

A poem tingles along the nerves (there is another line) when it is being written. A poet told me:

I have to write some things. Because I've been told to write them. Commissioned. That doesn't mean I mind writing them. It's writing, after all, and that's what I'm made for . . . In fact, 'commission' is one of my favourite words, I've got to live, I need my bread and wine and my sun like everyone else . . . a 'commissioned' review is better than good news . . . But the only kind of writing that tingles is poetry . . .

(Anonymous)

The reason poetry tingles in a way commissioned articles don't is because it has licence. The mind's eye requires freedom, if only in terms of a few minutes, in the cell of thought and feeling. As long as no editor has told me what to write about, and how many words I've got to do it, and what the style is that I've got to use, anything can happen when I write:

> The house opposite blows up while the surveyor reaches, with tape measure, from the top rung of the ladder . . .

> The grass is red as the sea's viscera . . .

> When I think of trees' trunks, I think of green, or lavender, or mouse-grey. Never, now, of brown. That's for telegraph poles . . .

But mostly, the power of free writing is to be seen when we think and feel about our relationships with people around us. A teacher wrote these notes on a course I was running:

> I was born in Cox Lane. That's gone now, they've pulled it down and it's a car park, Cox Lane car park . . . but whenever I park in that car park, I try to park on the site of the house where I was born . . .

Later, he read that piece of prose to us. And it was obvious that the relationships being explored were not only his with the car park and the road of his childhood, but his with us. As he read I thought of him as a pre-war child; and a week or so later, shopping in town, I tried to find the site of the house where he was born, so that, following his description of the place, I could park there.

Although I have used the word 'free' above, there was a cell in which this man was imprisoned as he wrote. I had asked him and his colleagues to write about an early memory *rigorously excluding any expression of feeling*. Paradoxically, it was this injunction, this cell, that led to the kind of writing, spare on the surface, that had emotional impact. Later this man gave us a further insight into himself, his upbringing, and the 1930s in general, as he added to his notes:

> . . . And I remember when I was nine or so. In the winter I used to have to take the wheelbarrow up to Derby Road to get the coal. It was cheaper if you collected it yourself, and on the way there was this pie shop, and I could smell the gravy, and I never had enough money left to buy a pie . . .

Here, this writer's mind's eye is looking with considerable intensity. An even more vivid example comes up later in this part: 'Quiet, quiet without my daddy here./ Quiet, quiet'.

So this third part is about the relationship between the individual child and his or her environment. It is also, as I've hinted above, about the relationship between two kinds of language. First, all poetry is essentially made of material at 'the advancing coalface' (O'Malley in Thompson 1969: 89). The indispensable condition of poetry is that what it is saying has not been said before. To choose an example at random, no poet is permitted to write about 'verdant pastures' because H W Baker has done so already, in his version of the 23rd psalm. As Pound put it more than once, 'make it new'. That is the reason for my Interlude on cliché. But the notion of new-ness goes beyond that. A new poem has to surprise readers, to delight them. By this, it shows that, as Barthes puts it (1982: 405–6), it desires the reader; draws him or her in. Only surprising language is seductive.

The other kind of language is the known, the already accepted. This is what Barthes calls 'an obedient, conformist, plagiarising edge'. It is too simple to say that this kind of language is wrong for poetry. The art has to have some language that is expected, or it would be unreadable. The diffi-cult and necessary thing is to make poems in which the two edges are both present in the right proportions. All of us have easy access to the sec-ond kind of language: we speak in its terms every day of our lives; it is there to make intercourse with the world possible. I am writing in that kind of language now. The first kind is much more difficult. It requires serious thinking to get to the coalface of language, and stay there for any length of time, and to push it forward.

Here is an example of language that is both conforming – this poem does not use any unfamiliar words – and surprising. The writer, eleven-year-old Pauline, has been asked to look at the stable where Christ was born through the eyes of a person other than herself, and she has chosen a bank manager (idea taken from Jill Pirrie's *On Common Ground* (1987)). After looking at reproductions of paintings of the nativity, she wrote:

> He enters the stable, briefcase,
> waistcoat and jacket,
> looking down at the baby,
> gold to his eyes.
> Joseph is singing 'A penny for a rhyme' .
> He looks at Mary crying with joy,
> her tears pound coins,
> the straw shreds of five pound notes,
> Jesus a fortune lying in a manger
> made of bronze, put together
> with silver shining needles.

....
Pauline, 11

While we reflect on these two kinds of language coming together, it's worth reflecting as well on what Pauline might be learning as she composes this poem. I speculate that she is thinking purposefully about four things: what a familiar, emotionally powerful scene might mean to a person other than herself (and, by massive extension, what this scene might mean to other human beings); what words and images there are that might express extreme joy; what phrasing and cadence she might use to express all this; and, given the word 'gold', what related notions she might come up with while reflecting on all this. In all this thinking, Pauline is learning about her language. Poetry has, because of its precision and integrity, this extraordinary power to teach us about words.

Chapter 8

Death and other obsessions

OTHER OBSESSIONS

The children in the following examples write about their obsessions. When they come into school, both at the beginning of their school careers, and at the beginning of each day, children know a great deal about the parts of the world that matter to them most. Also, youngsters of four or five have suffered: they have been lost in shops and argued with their parents; they have had tantrums and bad dreams; they have fallen out with friends; they have been bereaved of pets, or, possibly, relatives; they have been ill, and had accidents. But, although children come to school with all this ability, experience, passion and suffering, we as teachers tend to discount it, rather than build on it.

I have met children, in the past year, who are experts to the point of obsession in the following subjects: horse-riding, sailing, swimming, table-tennis, television soap opera, pop music, football, fantasy fiction for under-tens, the early stages in learning the violin, ballet . . . I have, while looking for Christmas presents, watched children examine with critical and appreciative eyes books on the solar system, dinosaurs, the human body. I have seen other children search CD ROM disks for the information they need, critically comparing one disk with another. I have watched children, who were known to be failures in school, fishing, with evidence of success. And yet this expertise has rarely, as far as I know, been used in school as a vehicle for learning, or as the substantive issue for learning.

This next poem was written by eleven-year-old Hazel. I had asked her, along with 40 other children, to write about something that obsessed her; something that was a passion. She told me her obsession was making jewellery, and (she went on) 'I can see how the finished jewels are poetic, but not making them'. This was an extraordinarily scrupulous observation. She could have taken what seemed to her to be the easy way out, and written about finished jewels, with all their easily-available poetic qualities of colour, shape, texture and association. But her integrity wouldn't let her: she identified her obsession as *making* jewels, not *wearing* them, and she was asking me, implicitly, if there was a way of making that activity 'poetic'. She wanted to write a poem about the relationship between herself and the materials and activities involved in her hobby.

This integrity is not unusual among children, unless it has been suppressed by an over-zealous need to please adults – teachers, competition judges, parents. All children have a need to get things right, to understand the situation, and to make sure we understand it too. A six-year-old girl appears in school red-eyed and pale. Eventually, after five minutes or so, she leaves her seat and comes out to me, more or less a complete stranger. 'I had two ducklings and a fox got them in the night.' As I begin to interrupt her with my consoling, she continues: 'He didn't want them, he didn't eat them, he just left them there'. In that sentence she is trying to get it true, and trying to make sure that I get it true as well. (This girl told me about the ducklings on the morning after Dunblane. There is unfathomable meaning there, I think.) This need for truth is the reason children will tell you about their parents' rows, and their visits to their step-parents: that is how things are, and however we as adults might want to make these things look different, children have a primordial need to tell the truth – or (this amounts to the same thing) their version of it.

I asked Hazel, the eleven-year-old, to write down a list of words to do with making jewellery that, she might guess, I wouldn't understand. She came up with: bugles, eyepins, earclips and long-nose pliers. I asked her about colours, and the feel of making jewels, and she readily listed other words, which I wrote down. Then I asked her to write an account of making jewellery that would give me a sense of what it felt like. Her first draft was no more than a brainstormed list, mostly nouns, with no main verbs, and a few adjectives. But to me it was vivid:

Eyepins, earclips, beads, tiny, fiddly, glistery, threading beads on to the wire, greasy in the middle, my hands all hot and sweaty, loop, long-nose pliers.

I asked her to find some groups of words that she liked so much she wanted them repeated in her poem. Here is her final draft:

Making Jewellery

Eyepins, earclips, shiny, new,
beads are my favourite,
rose red, grass green, any colour will do.
Bugles come in any shade but only one shape.
They're tiny, fiddly, hard to handle and small.

Eyepins, earclips, shiny, new,
Christmas is the best time to buy
when all the clips are cheap
and in the shops there's unusual beads
with glistery streaks.

I adore to see the beads spread out
like leaves in fall.
I thread beads on to the wire.
Eyepins, earclips, shiny, new,
turquoise, magenta, any colour will do.

I must have satisfaction before I clip off the wire.
Bending the wire is the hardest bit.
The long-nose pliers smell of metal
and they're greasy in the middle.
My hands are hot and sweaty
trying to get the loop just right.

Eyepins, earclips, shiny, new,
blues and yellows, any colour will do.

....
Hazel, 11

This poem has form, if not strict form. Hazel has achieved this by two simple devices. The first is the repeating lines 'Eyepins, earclips, shiny, new, / blues and yellows, any colour will do' and the second is the rhyme. Hazel has made the poem into a coherent whole with these two elements. She has used her language, and, in particular, these two devices, to build up her relations with the parts of the world she is already closest to. And the two lines 'I must have satisfaction before I clip off the wire. / Bending the wire is the hardest bit' capture deftly the obsessive passion of Hazel's behaviour.

In this poem by a keen fisherman, the images of the hook and the pond seem to take on a wider, and rather sad resonance:

Hooked

I'll catch you and feed you bait
But you won't be hooked.

I'll put you in my pond
But I can't catch you.

I'll protect you from bigger fish, so they can't eat you
But you won't let me.

I'll never fish again
But you won't be caught.

Why won't you let me?

....
John, 10

Most poets would say that it is impossible to write a real poem about anything that isn't an obsession. As teachers we are constantly trying to make the National Curriculum's chosen subjects obsessions enough for the children to make them want to learn about them by (among other ways) writing. An eleven-year-old writer, Tom, wanted to play Monopoly, he told me, but his mother insisted he did his English homework first, which was to write a poem:

The Chase

This cold damp day, the chase begins.
It starts to rain as I set up the Monopoly –
A loud splatting against the window-pane.
The dog is scared, waiting at Go
As a sleek Rolls-Royce rounds the bend.
The dice is rolled and spins off the board....
... It's eleven!
The poor dog pounds past: Old Kent Road, Whitechapel Road, King's Cross
    Station, The Angel, Islington
Where he pauses for breath.

Now he's on his way again, past: Euston Road, Pentonville Road; he doesn't
   stop at Jail, but finally reaches the safety of Pall Mall.
Slowly, sleekly the purring Rolls pursues the dog
But as he gathers momentum he's caught for speeding
And is sent, directly, to jail.

....
Tom, 11

Here is what Tom's first draft looked like: it is headed 'The Chase' and
Planning. The first line says:

The chase ~~began~~ begins one cold damp day;

and the line is changed to:

This cold damp day, the chase begins.

What follows next is unreadable, at least in my photocopy: a brief manic
flurry of crossings out and replacements. Then, 'a loud thumping' (this is
circled, and changed to 'spitting' in the margin) . . . and so on.

   This is an example of a child–writer bringing a home interest into a
school activity and being licensed to use its vivid jargon. But, more than
that, he is being allowed to make a creative shambles of drafts. I heard a
teacher in this boy's school complimenting a child on the mess she had
made of her first draft. How important this is! How respectful to a child
and her thoughts and feelings, to her abilities as a writer, to take seriously
the evidence of her learning in those first notes. And what a contrast (I confess) to my own ludicrous insistence on neatness, erasers and decorated
margins throughout the first quarter (at least) of my teaching career.

   Finally, this poem is a kind of primal act: it is an act of naming. 'Old
Kent Road, Whitechapel Road, King's Cross Station, The Angel Islington . . .
' means for this boy a game. In making this list, he relives a pleasure, and
establishes again an ownership over it, like Adam and Eve naming the animals. But his list vibrates in other minds in different ways: for a Londoner
living somewhere else now, it is a nostalgic hint at old journeys. Other lists
tell us stories about ourselves and our world, and how we live in it, and
think and feel about it. Listen hard, for example, to the names of coastal sta-
tions in the weather report. At least two poets (Seamus Heaney in *Field
Work* 1979: 39 and Carol Ann Duffy in *Mean Time* 1993: 52) have made res-
onant poems out of them. Or ask children to list their names for 'a gentle

rabbit': 'Floppy, Charlie Brown, Aaron, Gismo, Charlie Chalk'. Or for a rough one: 'Cross, Mad, Big Bunny, Heidi, Thumper'. Or for a tired one: 'Lazybones, Sleep, Snory, Sleepy-head, Comfortable' (five-year-olds). We all know that slightly neurotic feeling that a list – of things to be done before lunchtime, for example – is comforting. This is because, I suspect, each list in its strangeness asserts our ownership of things, our own personality.

The next activity shows children naming, again. Edwin Morgan (whom I quoted in chapter 5) has written a poem (*Poems of Thirty Years* 1982: 187) where he explores his own feelings about what appears to be an arbitrary list of things: dormice, rain, scent, newspapers, philosophy and so on. The pattern of Morgan's poem has been copied here by seven-year-old Malcolm. This boy had so far (I was told) refused to try any writing at all in school. He dictated this to an adult who wrote it down:

> What I hate about custard is its lumpiness.
> What I love about school is learning.
> What I hate about the sun is its heat.
> What I love about chocolate is its lovely taste.
> What I hate about football is losing.
> What I love about reading is its excitement.
> What I hate about cats are their muddy footprints.
> What I love about dogs is their warm fur.
> What I hate about my dad is his loud voice.
> What I love about my dad is his bouncy belly.
>
> ....
> **Malcolm, 7**

The boy handed this to me with an elated smile. He had made something with shape, vigour and feeling, and his poem had delighted his teacher.

Incidentally, what he had composed here is not only a valuable poem but also a useful reading book, both for himself, and for his friends. His text is certainly more vivid and more relevant to children's current concerns than anything about villages with three corners, or whatever. It also has that indispensable condition of reading schemes, repetitions: 'What I love . . . what I hate . . .'

Samantha, who was eight years old, wrote, among other things, 'What I hate about Christmas is when you put tights out and Santa only fills one leg'. With this work, one glimpses briefly genuine concerns that are difficult for us to see in any other way. 'What I love about books is you never miss any parts when you need to go to the bathroom' wrote a twelve-year-old girl, Megan, in a US Forces school. And, as one of her classmates wrote ('substitute' is American English for 'supply teacher'): 'What I like about substitutes is they don't know what to do'.

Another child used this simple format with relish:

> What I love about violins is their shape
> What I hate about violins is their sound
> What I love about my uncle is he helps me
> What I hate about my uncle is he takes games over on the computer
> What I love about my mum is she buys me presents
> What I hate about my mum is saying goodbye to her
> What I love about lions is their mane
> What I hate about lions is they eat meat
> What I love about animals is they are sweet
> What I hate about animals is they die
> What I love about clouds is they are white
> What I hate about clouds is they rain

....
Chauntelle, 9

All this work rocks quickly between ordinary ('What I love about chocolate is its lovely taste') and serious thought ('What I hate about my mum is saying goodbye to her'; 'What I hate about animals is they die'), just as life does.

DEATH

I have written about animals already in chapter 6. I want to explore here how pets, both at home and in school, are capable of teaching children something about one of the most potent aspects of their existence, and their relationships with the world: death. 'What I hate about animals is they die' a child wrote in one of the examples above, revealing in a sentence what we already knew: that children have to reflect on death. And yet all too often we protect them from experiences that would help them intensify this reflection. I have written elsewhere (1994b) how sometimes teachers have replaced a dead classroom rabbit with a similar live one rather than face the questions about where the rabbit is now.

These children used the technique described on p 54 in chapter 3 to write about lost pets:

Where's the goldfish
I looked at
when I was four?
Down the toilet.

Where's the puppy
I looked after
when I was seven?
We took it to Wood Green because it tore the wallpaper.

It is commonly supposed that the great unmentionable is sex. But what offends more in polite conversation is death. And yet even very young children reflect on this subject, as they must. Their grandparents die, their pets die; and sometimes, tragically, their parents, or even siblings, die. My son, when he was three years old, asked my wife, as she was dismantling his pram to put it in the loft, 'Are you putting that away for when I'm a baby again?' I believe that this was an example of thinking about his origins, his life and his death. It was evidence of profound thought.

If children are fortunate, they experience death in the literal sense first through their pets. In the following examples, the teacher I was watching read the children a short poem about the death of a pet rabbit. She pointed out that the poem had a repeated line; that it ended as it had begun, the last line echoing the first. She asked the children to write:

short poems about pets you loved that had died. Perhaps you could put some of these things in it: a phrase someone used about it – maybe something one of your parents used to say; a repetition; some descriptions of it . . .

Tiffany

Tiffany was sixteen,
Tiffany was old
But all the same
I got attached to her.
Now she is gone.

She was a beautiful cat
My mum always said.
She answered every question
With a bellowing miaou.

She was black and white
With a white chin.
We took her to the vet once.
He said 'She will live to twenty'.
I was very pleased.

But one day she wouldn't eat
Because her teeth were bad
So she stayed overnight at the vet's.
They found a lump in her throat.
They said it was cancer.
My mum agreed to put her down.
I knew her all my life.
She always loved me
Even though I snipped her whiskers off
When I was three.

Tiffany was sixteen,
Tiffany was old
But all the same
I got attached to her.
Now she is gone.

....
Sophie, 11

Normally, writing in this classroom was preceded by a hum of conversation, but on this occasion there was a silence. The children wrote with intense
concentration because they were staring into the void. I have already quoted
Emily Dickinson's lines: 'I like a look of agony / Because I know it's true'. I
need them again here. The reader is convinced of this writer's sincerity
because in the silence she is having to (or choosing to) write about lumps
and cancer, about love and death, and the price we pay for writing about
such things is that we cannot but be honest. In planning and producing the
third section, Sophie has moved away from the cheerful optimism of the
vet's remark through a great lesson about mortality – the cat's, of course, but,
by extension, everyone's, including her own – to a kind of resolution, a temporary stay, as Robert Frost would say, against confusion. There is evidence
here of a quiet desperation to get matters on the right footing. And, impres-
sively, the poem largely avoids the sentimental, even putting on record a

babyish act of unknowing cruelty. Sophie decorated her first draft of this poem with a drawing of the cat and the words 'In loving memory' to make clear to herself and to us the importance of what she had written.

Other children writing during the same session wrote memorable and telling phrases. Danielle remembered how her father used to say that the ducklings her pet duck had produced 'looked like little tulips', and after the death of her rabbit, Whisper, Michelle found everything was 'as quiet as a deer'.

Coco

Now he's gone
every sunny evening
I watched his
eyes shining in
the sunset.

now he's gone
in the summer
I remember feeding
him hawthorn leaves
from the hedge.

now he's gone
every morning
in winter before
I went to school
I melted his iced
up bottle so he can drink.

now he's gone
I remember the
tears leaving my
eyes when my
mum told me
he was dead

now he's gone
at least it

could have been
someone else's
rabbit

now he's gone

....
Michelle, 10

This last example is honourable for a frank admission at the end: it wouldn't have been so bad had it been someone else's rabbit. The line that the writing makes between the child and the dead animal is the most powerful of lines concerned with learning, first because death is such a powerful subject, and second, because it is mixed here with love. This writing changes the child so much, and education is essentially about change: it is a transformative experience. Children are capable of mourning animals that adults write off without a thought. The important thing is we should not write their poems off because we cannot empathise with their feelings. This next example is by an eleven-year-old boy, my son. He was on a school journey when he had an experience that he later recalled in a poem he wrote in his own room at home:

Snail in Hunstanton

The snail as innocent
as the Birmingham Six
has come out to damp itself in the rain
and we
the giants on the school trip
have walked down to the dark beach
with anoraks and wellies.
I am the unlucky one to step on it.
I look back and see it there dead.
I feel hot salty tears stinging my eyes.
Carl (one of us) cracks a joke
about three men
but all I can think of is the snail.

....
Daniel, 11

His teacher, who had taught Daniel to write poems almost every week in a previous school year, should feel encouraged because this practice had led to the boy using poetry in this way, in his own room, at home: in life, as it were, as well as in school. In this poem, I note how the tense changes in the middle ('have walked . . . I am'). This is a technique used by some of the speakers of the old ballads, who used it to heighten tension at the critical moment.

Chapter 9

'The stamping rocks and the squeaking birds'

Fantasy

I WISH I COULD PAINT

The children in this chapter have been set free to write unusual sentences. The teacher has shown them a picture by Chagall, and pointed out he paints impossible things: lovers flying on horseback, scarlet cockerels against a bright sky, dreams, monkey-judges . . . John Cotton has written a poem, 'Chagall', in which he explores more of these images (Sedgwick 1994a: 2). In writing about what impossible things they would paint if they were set free to do so, children explore their relationships with the world around them in all its joys and griefs. Here are extracts from poems by ten-year-olds:

> I wish I could paint
> the sound of the stars glowing
> the smell of the wind blowing in my face ...

> I wish I could paint my Grandad back
> because I never saw him ...

This next one captures some of the flavour of Chagall:

> I wish I could paint
> a stork carrying a baby in its beak
> flying over Mars with a star behind it
> and a cat doing a moonwalk on the moon ...
> a tiger in a field eating a hand.

> I wish that I could paint
> A man playing football in the Queen's palace.

I wish I could paint
A baby in the middle of the road
Crying because he's been kicked out of the house . . .

Some children vary the repeated line:

I can paint a picture of
flowers trembling towards the sun,
the sun sucking the water up . . .

'I wish I could.' That sentence explores an ordinary need in ordinary language: 'I wish I could have an ice cream'. The alteration to 'I wish I could paint' adds a strangeness. It enables the child–writer to focus the need on more emotional, if not spiritual questions. It also brings in another medium. The rest of the formula – the requirement that the need should be an impossible one – helps the writer to write sentences that are unique; sentences that have, quite possibly, never been spoken or written in the history of the human race before. It opens the door to images – terrifying ones, like that 'baby in the middle of the road / Crying because he's been kicked out of the house'. It leads to science and surrealism: flowers trembling towards the sun. It leads, of course, to death: 'I wish I could paint my Grandad back / because I never saw him'.

Jeanne, released (to her surprise I imagine) by the technique, wrote:

I wish I could paint the stamping rocks and the squeaking birds and the
juicy orange the twisting keys and ticking clock and jumping blood smashing
egg the ringing bell and slamming gates splashing sauce yawning man
crashing sea the twirling fish

Later she re-drafted the poem, following advice that she might think about where her lines ended:

I wish I could paint the stamping rocks
and the squeaking birds
and the juicy orange
the twisting keys
and ticking clock
and jumping blood
smashing egg
the ringing bell

and slamming gates
splashing sauce
yawning man
crashing sea
the twirling fish

....
Jeanne, 9

Here, a gusto in her use of language is far more important than any aspects of that language that might be easily measured, such as the use or misuse of full stops. The teacher present in the classroom and I were impressed by the verve of the half-finished, incorrect, abandoned poem. Whatever has she been watching / reading / dreaming? Who can say? Somehow she had discovered the power of lists, and present participles.

THE WORLD UPSIDE DOWN

One way to learn about the world and our problematical relationship with it is to view it upside down. Elsewhere (in my note on writing about the human-made environment) I have suggested that child–writers look at bicycles in this way. Making machines unfamiliar makes them clearer. And it is vital to see our relationship with the world as sometimes spiritual or surreal, or at a slight angle in some other way. Otherwise, everything would make sense! In their handbook *Catapults and Kingfishers* (1986) Corbett and Moses suggest using Adrian Henri's poem 'Tonight at Noon'. I don't need to quote it in its entirety: the title and this next poem written by an eleven-year-old under the influence of my reading of Henri will serve:

At Christmas in July
Millionaires will live on the streets.
Cats will chase dogs and
Birds will kill cats.

At Christmas in July
When you build a house you put foundations in last.
The grass will grow down from the clouds.
People will write with their feet and
Wear shoes on their hands.

At Christmas in July
When you play football you score own goals.
Everyone reads backwards,
People will live in the clouds.
People in shops will pay you to shop but then
You get your stuff free.

At Christmas in July
Pets will own us.
There will be an Atlantic channel from here to America,
The world will turn square,
The planets will turn together to make one big planet,
The rain will come out of the ground and rain upwards.

At Christmas in July
The world will be clean.

At Christmas in July
You'll say you'll marry me.

....
Jackie, 11

The ending stems from the fact that I pointed out to the children that, after all the impossible, topsy-turvy things in Adrian Henri's poem, it ends with what the speaker in the poem thinks is the most unlikely event of all: 'You will tell me you love me/Tonight at noon'.

Children can write genuinely disturbing lines under the influence of Henri's poem. Jade, for example, has written:

When we sleep in coffins and the dead sleep in beds
and tables fly
my pets will never die.
A poem will write me.

When we sleep in coffins and the dead sleep in beds
Hitler will come back and chop off our heads,

the knights of old will come back from the dead,
all our food will turn to lead.

When we sleep in coffins and the dead sleep in beds
Tippex is black,
the rules of football are to hack,
the queen lives in a wooden shack.

When we sleep in coffins and the dead sleep in beds.

....
Jade, 10

MAGIC: USING CHARMS

This is a way for children to approach the mysterious, and, at the same time, to use rhyme. Auden tells us in his *Collected Poems* that poetry is magic (that's why, he says, Christians should write prose). Children, being closer to the previous world than we are ('trailing clouds of glory'), and, as I've said before, desperate not to get things wrong, know that this is true. I asked a class of ten-year-olds to write a charm to get them through a problem that they feared, and I suggested that they could use one rhyme, and one only. Jonathan broke the rule (well done, Jonathan!) and used two:

To get rid of an illness

Lord I pray
That every day
You check I am not dead.
Give me courage, strength and health
Whilst I lie in bed.

....
Jonathan, 10

Chapter 10

'Where do you come from?'

The humanities

I worked for a week in a school where all the children were white. Paula Sorhaindo, who comes from Dominica in the Caribbean, was working in the same school. She told me that as she sat down with a reception class that morning, a child had asked her: 'What planet do you come from?'

Traditionally in infant classrooms most teachers have concentrated on teaching children about the familiar – the milk delivery, the post, the nurse, the doctor. But children are citizens of the wider world, and they need to meet, early in their lives, cultures different from the street where they live. The following example is made up of contributions from six-year-old children beginning to build a relationship with an African carving, and, by extension, with its maker, and the people that maker lives among. I spoke to the teacher:

> It followed on from an art lesson. They had looked at and talked about African statues made, mostly, of ebony. I said to the children, we're going to try and find out about this lady. It was a small group, they were going and coming. It was very informal. One boy came in, then went away saying 'That's boring!', came back, and eventually said some really good things . . . They were all uncertain at first. 'She can't talk, she's not real she's a statue'. I told them, 'we are going to pretend, we are going to fly to Africa, and we'll go in a jeep, and we'll see this lady in her village – what would we ask her? What questions would we ask her?' We had a map of Africa there, from a children's atlas, so it had pictures of people doing things on it. We looked at names of countries and flags. Gradually they started asking basic questions. 'What language do you speak? Where do you live?' Then Courtney asked again about the names of the countries. Then she said: Are you from Egypt or Mali or Sudan?
>
> We passed the statue around and other questions came out of the circle. How light is the sun?, for example, and 'Do you eat cherries?' Diamonds came early, from the picture of the miner. Every so often I read them back what they said so far. I was wrong once or twice. When

> Joanna said 'How light is the sun?' I said, 'Do you mean, how hot is the sun?' and she said, 'No, how *light* is the sun . . .'

How often what we see as a helpful piece of teaching is the opposite: it is, as here, the mere replacing of something imaginative with something conventional, something ordinary. As adults, we all too often replace the unexpected, with our instinct for the conventional, with something expected:

> It wasn't easy at first. They shrugged at me. 'What do you mean?' You have to guide them without influencing too much.

Crassly, I asked the teacher what National Curriculum attainment targets she was hitting, or aiming at, or whatever you do with such things:

> I wasn't aiming at any one of them! Children don't learn things to suit attainment targets. Geography, English, art are all going on here, of course, but the thinking is human, holistic. I think you're showing them, by writing their words down, that you value what they're saying . . . Is there anything in the National Curriculum about showing them what they say is important?

Later, the teacher and a group of the children wrote the sentences down in an order they negotiated. The teacher asked them, which sentence would they like to see repeated? And they chose the line that became the title:

How light is the sun?

Where do you come from?
Are you from Egypt or Mali or Sudan?
What is it like where you live?
What language do you talk?
How light is the sun?

What are you stirring around?
Are you mixing up soup or making flour?
Is that stick heavy – and that baby?
How can you carry your baby
And cook your dinner as well?
Are your arms aching?
How light is the sun?

Do you eat cherries
And do you have patterned clothes?

What do you sleep on?
And what do you dig up from the ground?
How light is the sun?

What is your baby's name
And your husband's?
Have you got a Grandma?
Are you my friend?
Are you my cousin?
How light is the sun?

The teacher told me later that one of the children had said that she would ask the woman, 'Are you a Pakistani?', and the other children had laughed. This remark, and the response, demonstrated the urgent need to teach children, whether they live in multi-ethnic or all-white areas, respect for their fellow human beings. To confront difference, to celebrate it, as in the activity I've just described, is better than the sort of crisis management that merely responds to racist remarks and actions; and far, far better, of course, than doing nothing at all.

EXAMPLES FROM HISTORY

It is possible for children to write 'by the light of history' (as Alan Williams has put it in a letter to me). This work enriches the elements of the National Curriculum the class is studying, as well as their language. Williams goes on to say:

> A greater knowledge of history is acquired through various forms of writing and the writing is enriched by historical information and imagery. These children (years 4 and 5) became immersed in a world of history and imagination, and the written word became pure pleasure . . . were looking at the Romans in Britain; much factual information was available and it was relatively easy to get the children to look at evidence and to infer from it. Yet the impact of the imagination was to contribute to our appreciation of the kind of country and people that the Romans must have encountered . . . Our class reading at the time was Linda Upham's *The Bronze Dagger*. There is a short passage which describes the arrival of a druid in a village. We used this to encourage the children to write poems on the impact this man would have on a superstitious people . . .

Here is one of the poems:

The Druid

His eyes glared through my skull.
His arms bare and patterned with warpaint, he was a druid.
My eyes were glued to his bearded face ...
His face was gnarled and wrinkled.
He had a hunting dagger tucked beneath his belt.
His hair was spiky with lime and it was also white.
I wondered what was going on behind those brown eyes.
He had a bronze torc around his neck
He had an oaken staff, brown as leather.
His cunning face appeared to trickle through my brain and into my heart.
His secretive brain works easily.
He raised his arm high and yelled, alien-like and unknown.
I glanced up, and when I looked he had gone.
He had juggled with my thoughts.

Alan Williams pointed out how this work avoids stereotypes, those clichés, or templates, of personalities, and helps children to empathise with people from earlier times. The stimulus has been so powerful that a line like 'His cunning face appeared to trickle through my brain and into my heart' acts out its meaning. The verb 'juggles' in the last line conveys admirably the impression of having been manipulated mentally by a force far stronger than one's own.

In the next example, a boy writing about the First World War, and using the traditional cumulative model of 'There was an old woman who swallowed a fly', offers us insights, if we are patient:

1914

1914. A muddy battlefield.
1914. A muddy battlefield. Silence.
1914. A muddy battlefield. Silence. The crack of a rifle.
1914. A muddy battlefield. Silence. The crack of a rifle. A Sopwith Camel zooms overhead.
1914. A muddy battlefield. Silence. The crack of a rifle. A Sopwith Camel zooms overhead. Cries of a German soldier.
1914. A muddy battlefield. Silence. The crack of a rifle. A Sopwith Camel zooms overhead. Cries of a German soldier. German planes. A squadron.
1914. A muddy battlefield. Silence. The crack of a rifle. A Sopwith Camel

> zooms overhead. Cries of a German soldier. German planes. A squadron.
> Bombs plummet towards the terrified British troops
A giant explosion.

All wiped out.

This has all the marks of male–juvenile aggrandisement. But in the world in which he has grown up, in the world that he sees mirrored constantly on television, in the role-models with which he is presented, how can this boy not write like this at some point? The poem has extra power coming from its model, the traditional 'There was an old woman who swallowed a fly'. Also, it enables the writer to use the words from an obsession of his, as I've suggested in chapter 8; in this case, the language of the First World War.

In the next example, children wrote about history. I had asked these children to reflect on a figure from history, and put questions like: 'What animal is your person? What growing thing? Is s/he earth, air, fire or water? What kind of music is s/he?' (Idea adapted from Brownjohn 1982.) What follows are extracts from longer poems:

> She is a bee looking for honey,
> a beautiful rose, a dark red colour ...
> (Queen Isabella)

....
Karen, 10

> ... a deer grazing
> a sunbeam grazing on the sea
> a colourful plant grazing in the rainforest.
> My person is mostly made of earth
> because what he uses involves the earth.
> He is a very quiet piece of music
> which you can't really hear,
> a colourful red wine.
> (Monet)

....
Thomas, 10

He is a giant ordering people about,
a prickly bramble with thorns like brambles.
He is air and fire because he howls in agony and burns in agony.
He is a table as still as the night.
He is a dark musty room full of rats and mice.
He is volcanic music burning with life.
He is deadly poison.
(Rameses)

....
William, 11

Sarah gives away her subject with her first line:

He is the hottest, sunniest, sandy, dusty day in Nazareth.
He is the most beautiful cuckoo flying from each tall refreshing tree.
He is the most beautiful exotic plant in the world with big yellow petals.
He is made up of water, air, fire and earth because it makes such a well-
    made combination.
He is the most soft, classical music anyone could ever have made.
He is an exotic greenhouse with all the flowers in the world.
He is a cocktail with the colours green, purple and red. It is best tasting.
He is a marble table with wood carvings hand-made with beautiful patterns.

....
Sarah, 11

Any adult objecting to cuckoo might reflect on Jesus's place in a human
family. It emerges vividly from this that Sarah, to use a Christian cliché,
'loves Jesus'. In this poem, the writer gives that love truthful, innocent
and powerful expression: 'water, air, fire and earth because it makes such
a well-made combination . . .'

Chapter 11

'You are the beautiful snow that falls in Nebraska'

Writing about love

Love and do what you will

(St Augustine)

In Joyce's *Ulysses*, there is a word 'known to all men' that is central to the novel. That word is love. It is also central to every human concern: love of God, married love, filial love, parental love, the love of money, patriotic love, love of nature . . . We cannot get through a day without using the word, at least in our thoughts. It is:

> To regard with passionate affection . . . To regard with the affection of a friend . . . To regard with parental tenderness . . .To be pleased with . . . To delight in . . . To regard with reverent unwillingness to offend
>
> (Johnson's *Dictionary*)

The largest personal, social, moral issues loom when children start to write about home and loving relations. Children should be doing this from a very early age. For all of them at certain times, and for some of them most of the time, domestic relationships are problematical. Sometimes the problems present themselves in terrible ways. We only have to read the Home News pages of our papers to appreciate the enormity of private terror. More often the problems are relatively trivial, but they are still problems that gnaw at children's self-esteem, and at their ability to live as social beings. And, because of their honesty, we can learn much – sometimes more than we want to know – about family life, by listening to children's talk and reading their writing – especially their poems. I remember a girl showing me a piece she'd written in response to the stimulus I've called 'Where's the – ' in chapter 8:

Where's the dad
I love
all the time?
Living in Halstead.

The next part of this book is about offering children chances to celebrate and mourn elements in their life with their families.

All the writing here, it should be noted, is about the most important aspects of our lives, and there are huge ethical questions to do with the way we should respond to it. Indeed, it is arguable that we should sometimes help a child make a piece of writing secret, if s/he has exposed feelings and events that might cause embarrassment later. Some teachers encourage children to keep a notebook which the teacher doesn't look at unless invited to by the child, and this practice teaches us two important things. One is that all writers keep journals; that a continuing notebook is a vital way of keeping the surface primed for the making of poems. The other is that we respect each other's privacy.

GIFTS

The seven- and eight-year-olds quoted in this first example had been asked to use a version of a technique described by Brownjohn (1982: 40). I told them about a poem I had written for my godson soon after his birth, and pointed out that presents don't have to be tangible objects: toys, teddies etc. I asked them, What would you give a baby you know if you could give him or her anything at all? The conversation that followed started with the ordinary: food, drink, blankets. But, under pressure of questioning, it soon took off:

A family poem

I will give you the north, south, east and west winds.
I will give you a poem that will say 'I love you'.
I will give you brown hazel eyes that shine in the moonlit sky.
I will make the sun and moon kiss and they will erupt into love.

....
Harriet, 7

If the last line seems a fraction over-written, it is worth considering whether children can ever learn to write appropriately if they don't take risks like this one.

To you

for Vidhu

I will bring you the tastiest fruits of India, guavas and mangoes.
I will bring you the cheekiest monkeys in the world.
I will show you the exotic colours of Africa.

....
Sumit, 8

Other children in the group wrote about giving baby sisters, brothers and cousins:

> a sheet of waterfall colours . . . pictures of Monet's waterfall . . . a wild deer with pricked ears to hear with . . . the sound of whales . . . the care of God . . .

Many of the images came into their heads from the walls of their class-room, on which there were authentic-looking imitations of several pictures by Monet and a display about water, their current topic. Their environment and my questions had led the children to think about loved babies. I believe this writing contributes to the relationships described in the poems, because it forces the children to think and feel with greater intensity than is perhaps usual.

MEMENTOES

I wrote a poem about my son Daniel when he was seven years old. It's about an experience nearly all parents remember: your child has spent a night away from home for the first time. The space, and the freedom to go to the pub or the curry house is wonderful at first. But then you miss him, or her. And even the irritating things they do seem endearing. The poem is spoken in my son's voice, and simply lists all the things in the house that remind me of him: piles of Asterix books, Appletize, Tomato Ketchup, Cocopops, chocolate spread, photographs, drawings. The poem is col-lected in Cotton and Sedgwick 1996: 15.

I have said before that objects comprise an objective correlative for the emotions felt about the person we associate with those objects. Make up your own list for a person: a particular Sunday newspaper, a brand of cigar, or beer; a composer, or an artist, or a singer. The phrase 'objective correlative' is Eliot's, and however much it sounds like jargon, it has been useful to many people in showing how distance takes the sentimentality out of poetry, and strengthens the feeling the poem stimulates (or strengthens the poem the feeling stimulates, or feels the strengths the poem stimulates). It also now looks like an over simplification as a description of a poet's methods, but it still has some use for those of us concerned with helping children to write.

I can best show the power of attempts at objectivity in writing by quoting the end of Hemingway's novel *A Farewell to Arms* (1935: 256). The hero has seen the body of his mistress who has died in childbirth: 'It was like saying good-bye to a statue. After a while I went out and left the hospital and walked back to the hotel in the rain.' Imagine a film version of this scene – I think there is one, but I can't be sure – where the hero half staggers, half tumbles down the hospital steps, his hands over his face; tears pouring over the knuckles. Rachmaninov – probably a piano concerto, near the end of the last movement – strides tearfully over the soundtrack. Which is the more emotional and which the more sentimental version? My contention is that the objective correlative of the rain makes the novel's version moving and vivid. It leaves us, as the readers, something to do; while the film version treats us like fools who need all the emotions spelt out for us, who have nothing to offer.

Curiously, my son was offered a similar stimulus as I had offered myself when writing about him. When he was eleven, he wrote this poem about me with his teacher John Lynch in 1992. Again, note the objects that stand for his feelings about me:

Dad

I taste your taste
when I taste a thick-topped mushroom pizza.
It reminds me
of me and you in Egypt
looking at the pelicans.
I listen to you
when I hear keys jangling
down on to the sideboard
where the phone is
or when I hear jazz swing
on a radio.
I see you in a book
of W H Auden poems
or when I see our stereo

left unattended in a corner
or a clean short
just out of the wash.

Children of all ages can use this objective technique. One boy has cheerfully written: 'My mum like[s] my grandads last bottle of beer' and in a sentence he has nudged innocently against his mother's feelings for her father, and his for her. Another child has written:

My mum smell like a rose.
My dad's arm is like a smooth papper.
My gran dad's arm's is like a rough pillow.
My dad's eyes are like drak [dark] choclete.
My mum's hair is like a black oil.

There is a corrected version of this poem in chapter 2. Here I would note that some of the grammar here is correct – the possessive apostrophes, for example. Should we then go for the rest in such an emotionally charged poem? Another boy hears his father 'in the beat of a Billy Fury record' (Sam, 10). This next writer writes in a notebook whenever he wants to. He had returned from a visit to his grandparents when he scribbled this quickly in his notebook:

My grandad's hands

Your hands are crippled old men moaning,
broken by steelwork,
covered in a shell of tobacco-smelling grey skin.
The rough joints swell to hurt you.
Their job is filling in a betting slip or
flicking channels on the TV.

....
John, 10

Six-year-old Charlotte was writing about anger when her late grandmother came to help her:

When I go angry I see the face
of my grandmother to remind
and I feel sad.

And I forgive the person I was
angry with.

....
Charlotte, 6

YOU'RE THE TOPS

Years ago, I helped to interview a teacher for a post in a school where I was headteacher. I had noticed that she had written 'Folk Dancing' in the box on her application form that asked about personal interests. This was a place that is usually used for 'walking', 'travel', even 'stamp-collecting'. I asked her if she had ever used this interest in a school, and she reacted with some surprise. It was clear that she felt it important to separate her professional from her personal life. But I have always found it difficult to maintain this barrier. And, indeed, there are, I suspect, two kinds of teacher: the technician who sees him/herself as a different person in the classroom from the one s/he is in the kitchen or the public bar or on the terraces; and the teacher who never thinks seriously about the gap between her or his private and professional lives, until the two come into noisy conflict.

I have long had an interest in popular American song, and have used jazz, for example, in work on anti-racism (Sedgwick 1994b). On more than one occasion I have found song helpful in the teaching of both poetry and the subject of the song. Once, as I was driving over the Severn Bridge to work in a school in Wales, Cole Porter's 'You're the tops' was on the radio. Now, songs are strenuously protected by copyright law, and so I can't quote the song here, but you probably know that it compares the beloved to all sort of strange things.

In the morning, I told a class of ten- and eleven-year-olds about this song, and read them the first draft of a poem I'd written the night before that went along the same lines. We talked about what 'obsession' means, and I asked them to write about the things that mattered to them most.

To Dad

1   You are the goal against United.
2   When I'm with you I'm like a brand new player.

3   Without you I'd lose to Stoke City.
4   You are the screams of Anfield
5   and the manager of the house.
6   I love you like I love McManaman
7   You can make me score a goal.
8   You are the star player in my life.
9   Without you I'd get lost on the pitch.
10   If it wasn't for you I wouldn't have a kit.
11   You are the FA Cup shining like a star.
12   I run through the tunnel and touch you for luck.
13   If you weren't here Liverpool would be relegated.
14   You are the mascot in my heart.

....

Eloise, 11

To Grandad

You are
an open flower
in the sunlight.
Without you
I would be
a dead rose
petals falling off me
When I'm with you
all the blossom
will bloom
When you're not with me
I'm a dead tree
chopped down
to the ground

lots of love Rebecca

....

Rebecca, 11

It was interesting working with this idea in a US Forces school, where the children used their memories and knowledge of, and feelings about, their home country. Avainte was ten when she wrote about her father:

You are
the beautiful mountains
of Colorado.

Without you
Florida
would be freezing.

You are
the beautiful sunsets
of California, the fantastic history
of Texas,
the beautiful snow
that falls in Nebraska ...

....
Avainte, 10

This is a simple but eloquent example of a child bringing to the classroom knowledge and experience that her current teacher (me) couldn't possibly possess. My role, after suggesting the structure that I've described, was to respect what she owned and understood. And in all classrooms, the teacher has that duty. To see what children know and understand above and beyond what we know is difficult to see except in unusual circumstances like these. I have merely thrown into relief here something we all ought to do, and rarely do. We routinely assume that any given classroom encounter is best established and enriched by the teacher and his or her knowledge and experience. What if it could be better established – and maintained – by the child–writers?

This poem is also, clearly, a moving celebration of Avainte's home country.

There are more examples of poems written by children with this stimulus behind them in Sedgwick and Sedgwick 1996b: 84–5.

SIX WAYS OF LOOKING

This way of writing comes (once again) from Sandy Brownjohn (1982), following Wallace Stevens who wrote a famous poem that was composed of 'Thirteen ways of looking at a blackbird' (Gray 1976: 33). This is a way of teaching children that the relationship between them and their world is often a complex one; that there is no simple way of perceiving anything; that different points of view, in all senses of that phrase, are all valid and, indeed, enrich our experience of the world.

My Great Grandmother's ring

is like a rope
that is used out at sea.
My Great Grandmother's ring
is silver inside.
I can see
the numbers 925.
It's been in the family for years and years.
My mum had it when she was young.
When I look at it, it glistens so bright
like the moonlight.
It shines there on my middle finger.
It sits on my finger
day after day
waiting for someone to admire it.

....
Samantha, 11

This writer has worked under the discipline of, or in the prison cell of, a search for ways of looking at the ring. She has seen a metaphor for its shape ('a rope/ that is used out at sea'), the material it's made of, some numbers on it, its family significance, its brightness, and its importance for herself. The learning in this piece of writing encompasses language, obviously, and personal and social thinking about the centrality of our most important relationships. It is both cognitive and affective, and it is also immeasurable.

I don't remember how the next poem was written. I think I worked on mementoes, and this child wrote this poem later. It has some of the mysteries we expect from poetry and we can generalise from it to some of our own experiences. It serves to end this part by reminding us that children face large disturbing facts, that we as teachers have to help them; and that the writing of poetry has a function way beyond the decorative; that the imagination, the mind's eye, enables them to reflect on how things were, and are, and might have been:

> Quiet, quiet without my daddy here,
> Quiet, quiet.

> Fireman carries up and down the stairs.
> But now it's

> Quiet, quiet without my daddy here.
> Quiet, quiet.

> It's not the same, there's no more arguing
> But lots of crying
> $\qquad$ Because it's

> Quiet, quiet without my daddy here,
> Quiet, quiet.

....
Katie, 9

Finally, a technical notion will often enable a child to communicate with the world around her, as in this poem by eleven-year-old Claire. I have referred to strict form several times. Here, as in Hazel's poem about making jewellery, repetition provides the writer with a kind of form. Often we find that if a child can spend some time and thought working on a phrase that pleases her, she can then build around this a working poem. This is because that phrase, for the very reason that it appeals to her, speaks of her personality. Therefore it is likely she will be able to work with it. Also, because the phrase pleases her, it is likely to have a cadence that is both relevant to her needs and the poem's meaning. Its intonations and rhythms have a job to do.

The poem's tentativeness enacts what it's about: uncertainty and mild disappointment, and the structure imposed sets Claire free.

The noises in between

I could hear the sea,
I could hear it.
It's just because of the
noises in between.

I could hear the noises
of an invisible animal -
I wonder what they would be?
It's because of the noises in between.

I could hear the cries of a baby in the womb,
Well I could,
The noises of everyday life,
Those noises in between.

I would hear a bud opening,
A rose creaking as it opens,
I could hear it,
It's just the noises in between.

I could hear a crab in the sea,
I might do,
I could ...
It's just the noises in between.

I'd love to hear the sounds
from another world, well I could
It's just the noise is blocking me,
The noises in between.

I want to hear a baby tree
breaking out of his seed,
but I can't hear it
It's because of the noises in between.

....
Claire, 11

'Me and the rest of the world' was how I began this part, quoting Donne. '. . . never' (he continues) 'send to know for whom the *bell* tolls; It tolls for thee'. In this part, I have tried to show how children can see their relationships with the world as problematical, and then explore those relationships in poems. History and obsessions, love and pain and death: children know these as surely as adults do. And poetry is a potent way of exploring them, and for helping them to understand more profoundly each day what they already instinctively know: they are part of each other, and when the bell tolls, it tolls for all of us.

I have throughout the book so far quoted the views of poets, though not, for copyright reasons, their poems. In the next chapter I look at children listening to, reading, and responding to great poetry by Yeats and Shakespeare, among others.

Part IV

Chapter 12

Children responding to poems

'The colour came out of his eyes, and they went grey like pearls . . .'
(A six-year-old on lines from *The Tempest*)

Of course, books about teaching poetry were published before the 1960s. But they were concerned, mostly, with children listening to and reading poems, rather than writing them. Among a collection I made while researching a PhD thesis (trendily called 'Managing Poetry' and, it must be admitted, unfinished) I treasure a hardback snaffled from an adviser's office in 1986. Danby (1940) is full of insights into the ways we teach children to 'appreciate' (a central word that, in books like this) poems, but it contains almost nothing on how they might write them. This is typical of the genre in pre-1960s years.

Danby's 'Suggestions for further reading' offers titles of powerful books, often of studies, one might say, of how poetry and its complexities can make students more sensitive human beings; of how the study of English is central to their induction into adulthood. Other books are by poets (Robert Graves, Laura Riding, A E Housman). Yet others are forgotten, despite mesmerising titles (*Archetypal Patterns in Poetry*, for example). But, as far as one can tell, creative writing isn't an issue.

Even books that obsessive students like myself believe are central for anyone interested in children and poems contain little about children actually writing them. Hourd's *The Education of the Poetic Spirit* (1949) is a beautiful example. It discusses poetry's power to teach children (and, it needn't be said, us) and quotes a few children's pieces, on which she builds a complex and stirring argument based largely on Coleridge. But the idea of a class of children responding to a stimulus is absent; was yet to become fashionable. Nevertheless, in these books (and many like them) one breathes an invigorating air, made up of an understanding of both the necessity for our heritage to be open to all our children, and for an urgent complementary need for the education of the imagination. In an atmosphere generated by thinking and feeling like this, children in our schools today should be strong enough, first, to take on that heritage, and, second, to criticise it in their own writing; to test past assumptions against their own mental, emotional and intellectual experience. But it is apparent that the conviction held in pre-1960s that through writing the imagination would be exercised and taught needed to be made more explicit.

It also needed to be made more public. There is little evidence of that conviction in the words of pupils of those years, now in their fifties. Speaking to people old enough to have been at school during those years, I recorded a partial but telling account of the reality of most poetry teaching before about 1960:

> I remember, I must have been about ten or eleven, I was in the last year of primary school, the teacher, Mr B—- wrote on the board the first verse of Gray's 'Elegy'. I can recite it now. [Does so]
>
> Well, I loved it. I think my mother had said the lines to me once or twice, I'm sure she had . . . Writing poetry, that never came into it . . . I loved hymns. I thought that listening to hymns, and singing them, and reading poems, that was as far as it went . . . 'There were ninety and nine that safely lay/In the shelter of the fold/But one was off on the hills away/Far off from the gates of gold/Away on the mountains cold and bare/Away from the tender shepherd's care.' Those words were magic to me . . . But writing poems. No. We didn't do that.

Another correspondent told me that she had been asked

> to write a poem! Just like that! I think we'd read poetry, but we'd never even been asked to think about writing it. Make sure it rhymes, she said . . .

A third wrote:

> My first memory of poetry was being taught to learn 'Abdul Ben Adhem' off by heart. I could do it, like I could learn tables, it was nothing to do with intelligence, it was just all learning off by heart. And we had to learn 'Quinquereme from Nineveh' as well . . . Yes, I do like poetry now, but not because of that. It's probably because of hymns . . . The first time I was asked to write a poem was at college, this was in 58/59 . . .

A fourth correspondent hinted at a frequently-held perception of the subject when she said: 'Poets weren't normal people then. They were seen as doing something none of us would see any point in doing . . .' The de-familiarising role of poetry that I have referred to elsewhere has often led to an image of poets as people who stand out in society. This image is often encouraged by poets who claim that a romantic temperament does indeed give them justification for bigger appetites for food or drink or sex, or inconsiderate ways of behaving often connected to those appetites (see the novels of D M Thomas, for example).

In the middle of the 1960s, there was a change. The 'conviction that through writing the imagination would be exercised and taught' was made more explicit. The harbinger of the change was a handbook by Margaret Langdon (1961) which described a lesson in which Langdon enabled a class to write poems about a spider. 'The classroom technique', wrote Walsh (in Thompson 1969), 'is a simple one: the teacher creates in words a situation where emotion is generated, and the class writes in the grip of that emotion.' The change – it was by now more or less a movement – probably gained unstoppable momentum with Alec Clegg's timeless book *The Excitement of Writing* (1964). This anthology of children's work (not all poetry) from the West Riding of Yorkshire was accompanied by trenchant comments from Clegg himself and the Leavisite critic Denys Thompson. Leavisite criticism, with its emphasis on rigorous reading, on imagination, and on the centrality of the study of English, made a powerful mix with those notions surrounding 'creativity' that stemmed from the progressive movement of the 1960s. I call Clegg's book timeless because the children's writing will long outlast contemporary political and managerial initiatives. This poem, by a six-year-old writing in the years between 1960 and 1963, is an example:

Our Jane

Our Jane is two.
She plays with a boy and
she has white hair and
she has blue eyes and
she has a runny nose and
she can't talk and
she eats biscuits and
she's fat and
she pinched my biscuits and
she's got a bike like an old crock and
she plays with my train and
she's a monkey when the telly's on.
She plays about.
She plays up and down.
They let her.

That poem will outlast the educational administrators of the time just as, in a more serious way, the poems of the Russian poet Anna Akhmatova will outlast the Stalinist censors who suppressed her work throughout most of her working life; just as the children's writing in this book and in your classroom, reader, will outlast contemporary political press releases about education.

Following (and influenced by) Clegg, books about children and poetry tended to be about children writing poems, as my book mostly is. Marie Peel's *Seeing to the Heart* (1967), for example, is a missal for believers in 'the holiness of the heart's affections and the truth of the imagination'. The change was mirrored in books about secondary English: note especially work by David Holbrook (1964, 1969). I think this shift is an important democratic one, because it was caused by a greater awareness that children have something to say, that their voices need to be heard if there is to be justice in our world. It accompanied other insights among teachers and teacher–educators about children as active learners with their eyes, ears, tongues, fingers and noses alert, rather than as passive pots to be packed with facts.

Nevertheless, much of the material produced in this democratic atmosphere was no more than agitation and propaganda. During the 1970s and 1980s, I received many books for review that were made up of poems by children who had been preached at about the wickedness of, for example, racism. After I had finished with them, I threw them away, so I can't quote them here. I was frightened. Racism was horrible: I'd seen it in my street, in the news; friends of mine had been on the receiving end of it. I had learned that it is institutionalised (for recent examples of this see Sedgwick 1994b: 113–14). But given all this, why were poems about racism so inert? They didn't help me share, even in a distanced way, the experience of being abused because of my race. They didn't help me to participate in the writer's feelings. I felt hectored. Indeed, that inertness made the racism seem less bad: are these null things all we can produce in the face of, for example, Asian youths being attacked outside football grounds? These little things reduced poetry to slogans, and, by association, took racism as an issue down with them.

I remember poems from a competition on freedom that were composed in chatty free verse. They were all speech with no reason for line endings, and written out of no more than a uniform sense of moral shock. This only goes so far: children need to know what different people have said a poem is, and that 1960s' view of it as a vehicle for what I have called 'agitprop' is very partial. Children need a wide experience of poetry. This means, if we are serious about combating racism, and we are, we should look at poetry from cultures other than our own. This is necessary, first, for the sake of children's own writing, second, for the sheer pleasure of it, and third, to enable the children to understand their culture and other cultures that impinge on it. It also helps them to learn that poetry isn't merely current, but about the past and the future, and about lives lived now and then in all sorts of different cultures. Children are no longer just listening, or reading, as in Danby (1940). They are responding.

And this is the democratic way. This is the way that gives yet more exercise to the imagination.

LISTENING TO POETRY

First, children need to listen to poetry. Here is a group of five-year-olds sitting on a carpet at 11.40 one winter morning. They have been at various tables during the last half hour. Some were writing, some drawing, some painting. Four were making a model of a car with sellotape, cardboard, glue and paint. I asked their teacher Beth, 'Aren't you supposed to have a timetabled day?' and she replied that they'd had an OFSTED inspection recently, and 'they'd loved the way I run my day!'

   Beth has promised them 'some poetry before you go out on to the playground', and they have said 'Yessssssssss!' This teacher has worked against the grain of the cultural definition of poetry as something boring; something that people different from us, called poets, do. I asked how she'd engendered this enthusiasm:

> In a way, I didn't. It's there when the children come into school. Listen to their rhymes on the playground, their sense of rhythm. I just nurture what's already there . . . I don't know, I love poetry, I just love the rhythms of the stuff, I think (sorry if this sounds a bit tacky but I can't think of another way of putting it) I think I just have a passion for it. I can't think of many things nicer than sitting down with the children with some poems . . . I try to make it in a literal sense an everyday thing, we spend fifteen or twenty minutes every day having fun with poetry . . . I always read something very serious and something very light, and I always try to read something old . . . Something new isn't a problem these days, with the books published for children . . .

I had to ask Beth a question I myself am constantly being asked: How do you still find time for poetry in your overcrowded, legislation-enforced curriculum?

> If you haven't got time for poetry, it's like a Christian not having time for the communion . . . Anyway, I can find poems for any topic, in any subject . . .

She says to the children in a lugubrious voice:

> Old Abram Brown
> Is dead and gone –
> You'll never see him more.
>
> He used to wear
> An old brown coat
> That buttoned down before.

Old Abram Brown
Who's dead and gone
Was kind to Joe and me:

He'd tell us tales of men o' war
And guns that rolled at sea.

Old Abram Brown
Is dead and gone –
You'll never see him more.

Then there is a silence. The children look up, suitably solemn. There is, evidently, the need for something lighter. The teacher says, beaming at the children, that here is a poem about 'Mrs Toft' (one of her colleagues, a classroom helper who has just stopped cleaning paintbrushes at the sink, and who has perched on the edge of a desk to listen to the poems):

Our Mrs Toft is very kind.
She goes to church on Sunday.
She prays to God to give her strength
To smack the kids on Monday.

The children (though not, evidently, Mrs Toft) have heard this before, but they still find it funny. Then Beth turns to her impressive and cheerful looking collection of poetry books (see Appendix 2 for a list) and reads some Gerard Manley Hopkins: a writer not known as a poet for children. And though this is not one of his difficult, dark poems of spiritual pain, it is grammatically complex. But her enthusiasm, her skill, the poem's vigour and its strangeness carry the children through it:

Pied Beauty

Glory be to God for dappled things –
    For skies of couple-colour as a brinded cow;
        For rose-moles all in stipple upon trout that swim;
Fresh-firecoal chestnut falls; finches wings;
    Landscape plotted and pieced – fold, fallow and plough;
        And all trades, their gear and tackle and trim.

All things counter, original, spare, strange;
    Whatever is fickle, freckled, (who knows how?)
        With swift, slow; sweet, sour; adazzle, dim;
He fathers-forth whose beauty is past change:
                                        Praise him.

Second, children need to talk about poetry. 'What do you think couple-colour means?' Beth asks the children. She faces a sea of bemused looks.

'Well, what is a couple?' Tentatively Michael says, 'Two?' 'Yes!' says Beth. 'So couple-colour means –?' 'Two colours!' several children say. Then the discussion continues: 'couple like two is like two colours on a cow's back . . . like on a fish, when you've caught it, the different colours . . . I like the f's and the s's in the second verse . . . but look, there's lots of f's in the first verse . . .' It simply does not matter that children don't appreciate at this point that those f's serve to emphasise the connection with 'father's-forth' at the end, and that so many words in English with f's prominent in them are to do with fecundity and the power to make.

One mistaken view about children listening to poetry is the one expressed by people who think children can only appreciate easy verse; that only verse that uses words entirely within the children's experience is any use to them. And while it is true that much verse that is genuine poetry – nursery rhymes, playground rhymes and so on – is a real entry point to the understanding of poetry, it is also true, and less frequently appreciated, that (as George Whalley puts it in his article 'Teaching Poetry' in Peter Abbs [1989]):

> . . . even 'difficult' poetry is directly accessible (even though not imme-diately intelligible) to an untrained reader – as music is accessible to listeners untrained in the art of music . . .

This is a neat distinction between 'accessible' and 'intelligible'. I always thrill to the last movement of Sibelius' Fifth Symphony and to Chopin's Fantaisie Impromptu Opus 66, while knowing almost nothing about the technicalities of orchestral or piano music. The children here, who, this afternoon, will spend five minutes searching library books for 'couple-coloured' things, and, on their way home, the grounds around the school, have no notion of what Hopkins' 'sprung rhythm' is, or the psalms that this poem echoes, but it is 'directly accessible' to them though not 'imme-diately intelligible'.

LISTENING TO SHAKESPEARE

This has been a central discussion in the educational debate over the past few years, and anyone writing on teaching poetry can only applaud that fact. It is a truism to say that Shakespeare's language is woven into almost all our speech. 'Dying fall . . . mistress mine . . . sweet and twenty . . . cakes and ale . . . some are born great, some achieve greatness, some have greatness thrust upon them . . . midsummer madness . . .' These phrases from just one play, *Twelfth Night*, demonstrate that we are often quoting Shakespeare when we don't know it. More importantly, he provides for us, as he has for our ancestors, markers for our integrity. His facing up to things has given us example after example. The character of Hamlet exemplifies the human instinct for revenge frustrated by all kinds of moral anxieties. *Twelfth Night* holds a mirror up to our sexual ambivalences, our moral laziness, our cruelty, our shallow Puritanism, our vanity.

The problem has come about with an offensive sentimentalisation of Shakespeare and his work. Thus the Prince of Wales talks about the Bard and his heritage, apparently unaware of the reality of the moral implications of the plays and poems. Politicians of the right hi-jack him on the grounds of Ulysses' speech in *Troilus* that is about the importance of order, not recognising that Ulysses isn't an ideal man in any sense, but a foxy politician. And Rhodes Boyson says (see Rex Gibson in Styles and Drummond 1993: 77) that we should approach him through the distorting (and poetry-free) mirror of *Lambs' Tales*. These ways of pinning Shakespeare to a moment in our history, to a set of values that is now out of date, belie the fact that, as Gibson implies, you can't teach *The Merchant of Venice* before the holocaust in the same way as you can after it. Shylock the Jew in the Lambs' account is a stereotype that has taken on much greater offensiveness in our century.

Gibson has in his article several delightful accounts of Shakespeare in primary schools. And here, to demonstrate the truth of Whalley's remark above (Whalley 1989), are children in a large primary school speaking Shakespeare during assembly. The poem is one of Feste's songs (*Twelfth Night* Act 5: Scene 1):

> When that I was a little tiny boy,
>   With hey, ho, the wind and the rain;
> A foolish thing was but a toy
>   For the rain it raineth every day.
>
> But when I came to man's estate,
>   With hey, ho, the wind and the rain;
> 'Gainst knaves and thieves men shut their gates,
>   For the rain it raineth every day.
>
> But when I came, alas, to wive,
>   With hey, ho, the wind and the rain;
> By swaggering could I never thrive,
>   For the rain it raineth every day.
>
> But when I came unto my beds,
>   With hey, ho, the wind and the rain;
> With tosspots still had drunken heads,
>   For the rain it raineth every day.
>
> A great while ago, the world began
>   With hey, ho, the wind and the rain;
> But all that's one, our play is done,
>   And we'll strive to please you every day.

The headteacher says the odd-numbered lines, while the children to his left say the line 'With hey, ho, the wind and the rain' and those to his right say 'For the rain it raineth every day' – except in the last stanza, of course. Both the headteacher and the children emphasise the rhythm crudely, shouting rather than sighing 'heigh-ho' for example. The headteacher says his lines in a suggestive voice, and with appropriate actions. He swaggers and then staggers slightly in the third stanza, and mimes tossing off a pint. There's the hint of a hangover in the fourth. If this is crude, the headteacher says, another day they will discuss how the poem might be said differently, and then speak it more reflectively. On another they might listen to one of the many settings of the song.

Subtly or not, the children say their lines (and listen to their friends' lines) with evident enjoyment, even though the poem, or song, is full of terms ('man's estate', 'knaves', 'wive', 'swaggering', 'thrive', 'tosspots' and 'all that's one') that mean nothing to them. Indeed, far from cutting difficulty out from the poems we read to children, we should combine it with our expressive reading and acting (the headteacher toping, slurring and swaggering, for example) to show them what words mean. I labour the boozing because there is a tendency to weaken Shakespeare's poetry by forgetting that his work is concerned with lowlife – all our low lives – as well as kings and princes. This sentimentalising tendency often goes with calling him 'The Bard' or 'The Swan of Avon', and with seeing his plays as 'tales'.

Discussion of another song from Shakespeare shows how young children can respond to poems that they do not understand. 'Full Fathom Five' occurs in *The Tempest*, Act 1 Scene 2:

> Full fathom five thy father lies;
>   Of his bones are coral made:
> Those are pearls that were his eyes:
>   Nothing of him that doth fade,
> But doth suffer a sea-change.
> Sea-nymphs hourly ring his knell:
> Hark! now I hear them – ding-dong, bell.

Not only is this poem difficult in that it alludes to abstract ideas beyond the scope of most children's lives, it also describes a terrible experience, the death by drowning of a father. It sheds light on other poems some of the children will read – Eliot's 'The Waste Land', for example, and Sylvia Plath's 'The Colossus'. I gave a group of eight- to eleven-year-old children copies of the Shakespeare and asked quickly a few ill-thought-out questions: 'What's this poem about? What is a sea-change? What is rich and strange?' I wrote down some of their comments:

> I thought it was about a statue . . . There's been a shipwreck, you can tell because there are fish and there are bones, and there's pearls . . . Pearls

come in big clams . . . in oysters! . . . Yeah, oysters. This is something to do with the sea . . . Could be a river . . . I doubt it, look at the seaweed . . . Could be riverweed . . .? What is this sea change? . . . That's the tides, or it could be something has happened in the boat . . . Or it could be that he has died, and he has turned into a swarm of fish . . . I think somebody's father was a sailor in a shipwreck, and the sea change, is, the weather changed and he got shipwrecked . . . Rich and strange, that's the pearls that were his eyes . . . What's a knell? [several children grab dictionaries and feverishly thumb through them] It's a joint in the human leg, no, it's a bell rung for a death . . . Fathom means that she has found out where her father lies . . .

It is a shame that I didn't record the conversation properly, as in the next example. But even in these scraps, we can see learning moving along with pace and power at times, haltingly at others. The hypotheses made about the changes, for example, erratic as they are, will from now on influence my reading of this song and the play, as will the astonishing final sentence, where someone finds a double meaning for 'fathom'. 'Clams . . . oysters' shows how children can be relied on to teach each other.

Another group of children read the same poem. These eight-year-olds thought seriously about the word 'sea-change':

He's changed into a fish – No, he's changed into a skeleton! He got eaten, and the skin all came off, and he changed into a skeleton, his bones turned into coral – and his eyes, his eyes, his eyes (hesitation) under the water all the colour came out of his eyes, and they went grey like pearls . . . the sea colours all changed as well . . . I think the sea change is people putting their rubbish in the sea and making it all dirty . . .

'Under the water all the colour came out of his eyes, and they went grey like pearls.' If it is true that real poetry offers us something new every time we read it with attention, I was rewarded here with an insight simply by reading the poem, and listening to a child talking. Her frank unsqueamishness made Shakespeare's pearl image painfully clear to me. The fact that someone makes an anachronistic comment in his/her remark about pollution doesn't devalue the experience, any more than the erratic hypotheses I noted in the first transcript.

CHILDREN READING POETRY

The next example is an account of four six-year-olds in a Cambridgeshire village school responding to a poem by W B Yeats (1950: 44). I'd like to compare the seven-year-olds' talk with an institutional expectation. In front of me as I write is a copy of a now out of date *KS3 English Anthology* (Department for Education). It contains, as benchmarks for thirteen- and fourteen-year-olds, a strange mixture: predictable passages from Chaucer, Shakespeare, Keats, Clare, Dickens, Wordsworth, Browning, and Wilde; writers it is hard not to identify as token Blacks, or token women: Samuel Selvon, Dorothy Wordsworth, Doris Lessing and Elizabeth Jennings. Other writers are good ones, no doubt, but ones that might be chosen by anyone half-acquainted with the area. Anthony Thwaite, fine. But what about Geoffrey Hill? Patricia Pogson, but what about Fleur Adcock, or Anne Stevenson? One writer is token nothing: Derek Walcott, with his wrenching 'The Young Wife' (*KS3 English Anthology*) but why this writer among others? Who should choose?

   In other words, the anthology is an arbitrary one composed for, not the average *child*, the average *expectation*. Children deserve, and can do, much better. It all depends on what we expect them to do. In this example, Eddie, Thomas, Beibei and Jessica are talking about 'The Lake Isle of Innisfree'. The teacher, Jane Hodgman, of Babraham School, had read the poem to the children, and they had painted pictures of their images of the Isle. Then she started them talking, and left them with the tape recorder running:

E   'I will arise and go now'
T   I think I know what the first line is about. He'll go to the Isle of Innisfree . . . and he'll build, a cabin is a type of house made out of clay
B   or wood
T   and wood
E   and 'a small cabin build there of clay and waterless made'
B   wattles
E   'Nine beans in a row I will have there'
T   'Nine bean rows' is like he'll have nine rows of beans in a kind of a garden, or something like that
B   I don't know
E   Let's read it again, 'Nine bean rows I will have there' and have . . .
J   There's 'a hive for the honey bee'
E   to get honey from
B   yeah, the honey bee really eats the honey
E   and 'Nine bean rows I will have there, a hive for the honey bee, / And live alone in the bee-loud glade'
T   'live' [adjective] you said, it's really live [verb], but 'Nine bean rows', that's a kind of mystery
E   'And live alone in the bee-loud glade'
B   mystery?
T   nine bean rows nine rows of beans
B   Do you know, on The Crystal Maze, did you see –
J   Shhh
B   – the children's Christmas special? Crystal Maze. I didn't watch all of it –

E   We're looking at this poem here

T   'Nine bean rows'

E   'I hear it in the deep heart's core'

T   No 'I shall have some peace there' even though he's all alone, because he's all alone

E   'And I shall have some peace there, for peace comes dropping slow'

T   slowly peace comes

B   yeah there's always peace there

T   This poem's upside down . . . nine bean rows, nine rows of beans, that's upside down

E   so nine bean rows, rows bean nine

T   no not like that, nine rows of beans, nine bean rows

E   nine rows of beans, nine bean rows . . . 'I will have there, a hive for the honey bee'

T   a hive

E   'honey bee,/ And live alone in the bee-loud glade'.

T   because there's tons of bees buzzing round in the glade, and a glade is a kind of space in a wood

B   'And I shall have some peace there, for peace comes dropping slow,/ Dropping from the veils of the morning to where the cricket sings'

T   the cricket sings on his violin

E   look, so this man went to this island, 'Dropping from the veils of the morning to where the cricket sings'. I think the morning goes by 'to where the cricket sings' . . .

. . .

B   Let's read it . . . Where's Innisfree? Let's think about the place

J   It's the island, he calls it the island

E   it's in Ireland

T   and actually

B   it's inside a free, inside you're free everywhere

E   you're free everywhere and you can go anywhere on the island

T   But what about the first bit, what does Innis mean?

E   Inside this island, it's free on this island and if you go anywhere else you are stuck there and if you go to this island you're free

. . .

J   it's really noisy in the city and it's really quiet on the island

E   yeah and you're really free on the island

B   What's core?

E   Our heart is the core

T   The middle of our heart is the core

J   like the middle of the island

B   'I will arise and go now' (T tries to interrupt)

E   what's 'wattles made'

B   I don't know – (T tries to interrupt)

T   Excuse me it could –
J   It could be the veil of the leaves –
T   I know what 'rise and go' means! It means he'll get up and go back to the city
E   Then he'll rise up and go back to the island . . .

This is extraordinary, but not so much, I would argue, because of the talent these children display in their talk about this poem, but in the opportunity they have had to explore the words of a (to them) long-dead poet. I suspect that teachers have conventionally perceived children's imaginative powers as much smaller than they are. We look at children and view them in terms of a deficit model; that is, in terms of what they don't know and can't do. These children have been approached here with greater expectations. Let's examine what they achieve.

'The task of teaching literature', Benton *et al.* (1988) suggest, 'is an enabling one – to encourage children to become "keen readers".' They go on to point out a neat double meaning in the word 'keen' – children become both 'enthusiastic and committed', on the one hand, and, on the other, 'intellectually acute'. In the transcript above, four six-year-olds demonstrate very clearly that commitment. We can hear it in the passionate tone of voice, especially in Thomas's remarks, and when one of them, Beibei, tries to change the subject, she is quickly brought back to the point by the others:

B   Do you know, on The Crystal Maze, did you see . . . the children's Christmas special? Crystal Maze. I didn't watch all of it –
E   We're looking at this poem here

Four different personalities are exposed in these words. Eddie is an organiser, keen to get elements in this fascinating confusion tidied up. He constantly brings the conversation down to earth with a quotation, which we can tell he greatly enjoys. He also enables Thomas's stranger speculations:

T   Nine rows of beans, that's upside down
E   So nine bean rows, rows beans nine . . .

As the extract ends, Eddie has moved from being a quoter to being an interpreter. Thomas has dramatic, odd insights: 'that's a kind of mystery . . . nine bean rows nine rows of beans . . . the cricket sings on his violin . . . The middle of our heart is the core . . .' Sometimes he has to make a fuss to get his point across. Jessica is quieter than the others, but has an important role in bringing Beibei back to the point ('shhh' is probably evidence of a genuine frustration – she is totally involved in the conversation). She grows in confidence as the conversation goes on, eventually saying a beautiful line of her own ('It could be the veil of the leaves'). Beibei sounds mischievous at times, but her question about the television programme may well not be as irrelevant as it seems. It is probably connected to Thomas's idea of 'mystery'. Her growth in the course of the transcript (like Eddie's and Jessica's) is striking. Here the setting and poem are teaching the children about each other, and about other people they will meet in life who have similar character traits.

Notice how the children teach each other. Eddie's 'waterless' is corrected by Beibei, and later on it's the other way round as Eddie explains to Beibei the meaning of 'core'. When there is a difficulty, they suggest to each other ways out: 'Let's read it again . . . Let's read it . . .' and offer each other, with great fluency and insight, various interpretations of the poem. Indeed, these children are complicit in the creation of the poem. Many writers have shown how the old-fashioned notion of a poem existing on its own, unaffected by its readers, is a false one. We bring to every reading of a poem a huge baggage – our life histories, our memories, our temperaments, our current moods, our intellectual interests, our religion, our relationships, and all these are brought to bear on the poem as we read it. 'Every time a reader experiences a work of art, it is in a sense created anew', says Rosenblatt, quoted in Benton *et al.* (1988). She goes on to distinguish between the text, which is no more than the marks on the page, and the poem, which comes into being only when there is a rapport between reader and text.

To my mind, there is an analogy here with a single-seater aeroplane crashing and killing the pilot in the middle of the desert. The noise is the equivalent of that bare text on the page. It will never come to life – be heard – unless there is someone to hear it; at the lowest level, ear drums for the sound wave to hit. Indeed, without the human presence, it could be said that the sound isn't made; similarly with the poem that hasn't been responded to in the way these children have responded to 'The Lake Isle of Innisfree'.

But it isn't only the children who are teaching in this teacher-free setting. The poem is a teacher (as I've already hinted). The word 'teach' stems from the Greek word 'to show', and this poem is teaching, that is, showing, the children an island, and powerful ways through thought and, more importantly, feeling processes that would have been impossible in any other lesson. It shows the children what Thomas sees as the mysterious effect of the assonance in the line 'Nine bean rows I will have there, a hive for the honey bee', where the 'ee' sounds in 'bean' and 'bee', I would guess, were among the elements that made Thomas feel the poem was upside down. It shows the children the impact on the imagination of words like 'core', 'glimmer' and 'purple'. Of course, none of this teaching is measurable, and therefore it presents a problem to us when we are trying to plan and evaluate learning merely in terms of observable behaviour. Indeed, one of the most important functions of poetry (and this is true of all the arts) is to show us that what isn't presentable on checklists to managers is probably the most important aspect of our learning; that what can't be predicted in terms of learning outcomes matters more than anything else. This is because it can be secret, and subversive, and therefore immeasurably powerful.

We have in this extract from a longer conversation a detailed picture of relationships that are educational, social and affective (insofar as one can distinguish these three elements) between four children and a poem. As ever, the important action is in the lines between the elements in the group, because it is along those lines that the charges travel that produce the intense imaginative, intellectual and affective activity we can glimpse. We might usefully compare this activity with other common activities in infant classes: reading a scheme book, for example, with an adult, where the lines are fewer and infinitely less charged; or copying letters in a handwriting exercise, or painting disc after disc bright colours for the shields on a Viking ship.

CONCLUSION

There is, throughout this book, an unresolvable tension between restraint and licence, prison and freedom. At one end of the line, teachers give children traditional forms and ask children to write inside them. 'The notion that the child is a natural poet is a sentimental fallacy', as John Mole (in Bagnall 1973: 189) put it. He goes on to say:

> the way of encouraging the writing of poetry which I find the most rewarding is *formal*, in the best sense of the word . . . the classroom seems more relaxed and humming with invention when there are rules . . .
>
> (Bagnall 1973:196ff)

At the other end of the line, teachers attempt to set children free by simply writing from their feelings. The child is a natural poet. The classroom method in this case is to fill the classroom with emotion, to pump it up like a tyre, and to get the children to write in the grip of that emotion. I have tried to show that this is not a simple matter; that, indeed, writers need the prison of form and various traditional techniques in order to be free. I think it is true to say that all the children in this book are writing under restraints: the box, for example, or the form 'Where's the ——', though I think for young children, rhyme and strict metrics are less appropriate restraints than, say, alliteration and the use of repeated lines. Indeed, Mole's suggested formal shapes are less formal than you might expect, and resemble much of the work I have described in this book: 'Once I was . . .Now I am' for example leads to a telling poem:

Once I was water, a mere droplet
Trickling from beneath the stones

. . .

Now I am a brook, a burn . . .

Children also need to be taught by what poets have written before
them – poets that the tradition says (and that tradition is a powerful one)
are great: Shakespeare, Yeats and Hopkins, to mention those quoted above.

Children need strict form sometimes, and they need to scribble words
down in the grip of their feelings at other times. This is not to take the easy
way out, of insisting on balance, as though some middle way was always
right. It is to say that writing down the essential words that express an
emotion in some kind of tranquillity must often come first, while the car-
pentering, the making of the little stanzaic boxes comes second. There is
evidence that some poets – Philip Larkin was one – worked inside the
boxes from the word go but other poets wait till late for the freeing prison
of form. Reiterating Coleridge is the best way to end: 'more than usual
state of emotion . . . more than usual order'.

Hourd quotes the following from Coleridge's *Biographica Literaria*, and I
offer it again here because it is central to anyone concerned with the teaching of poetry:

> The poet . . . diffuses a tone and spirit of unity that . . . fuses each to each
> by that synthetic and magical power . . . Imagination. This power . . .
> reveals itself in the balance or reconcilement of opposite or discordant
> qualities: of sameness, with difference; of the general, with the concrete;
> the idea, with the image; the individual, with the representative; the
> sense of novelty and freshness, with old and familiar objects; a more
> than usual state of emotion, with more than usual order . . .
>
> (quoted in Hourd 1949)

One glimpses in Hourd the vigour of much that is under attack, and which
will not be defeated by current materialism: that is, the belief in the imagination both as a vision, and as the synthetic power that Coleridge
describes here. It is this quality that will, if anything will, enable us to sur-
vive the philistine years with our spirits intact, that will see the money
changers out of the temple of education, where they have taken up resi-
dence in the heart of the sanctuary. This quality is expressed in the way
children, first, talk about poetry: 'The colour came out of his eyes, and
they went grey like pearls . . .'

It is expressed, secondly, in the way they write it:

We are feeble ghosts/from the ageing years . . . My Mum's hair is like dark
oil . . . I was invisible through the remote lakes/ I was trying to act scarce . . .

I am the dragging of dead thrushes / across the garden ... I wish I could paint my Grandad back / because I never saw him ... His cunning face appeared to trickle through my brain and into my heart ...You are/the beautiful sunsets/of California, the fantastic history/of Texas,/the beautiful snow/that falls in Nebraska ...

For the children learning is a matter of paying attention to poetry, and writing. For us, as teachers, it is a matter of listening for the noises in between, and writing ourselves, if we dare. Alice and her friends have, I am sure, been my witnesses to these truths.

Appendices

This is an index of the starting points my colleagues and I have used to provoke children to write. I have described them, with examples, in this book. While all these triggers are useful in various contexts, we must bear in mind that children only become true poets when they write without the immediate stimulus of an exercise such as this. And they stay poets when they continue doing that. To be a writer is to write, obsessively, every day, with sometimes no more stimulus than the need to write. What follows are starting points, in two senses: they are starting points for poems, and they are exercises for the imagination of starter-poets.

APPENDIX 2

A Select Book list

This is a select list of books relevant to teaching poetry in the primary classroom. What comments I append are intended to be the briefest guidance.

Practical books for the teacher's desk

Sandy Brownjohn (1994) *To Rhyme or Not to Rhyme* Hodder and Stoughton

This is an omnibus edition of Brownjohn's first three books on this subject. When the first appeared (*Does it Have to Rhyme?* 1980) it changed my teaching. From what I gather on courses around the country, it was influential in many places. Full of good ideas, it enables teachers to free children by putting them in little cells of technique: syllabic counts, metaphors, and rhymes. The other early Brownjohn books are *What Rhymes with 'Secret'?* and *The Ability to Name Cats*.

Brian Moses and Pie Corbett (1986) *Catapults and Kingfishers: Teaching Poetry in Primary Schools* Oxford University Press

A primer more like a recipe book than anything else, with many tips for good classroom practice, and some useful poems to use as exemplars ('Warning' by Jenny Joseph, for example, and Adrian Henri's 'Tonight at Noon', a poem redolent of the 1960s). *Catapults and Kingfishers* was complemented in 1991 by *My Grandmother's Motorbike: Story Writing in the Primary School*.

John Cotton (1989) *The Poetry File* Nelson (originally Macmillan)

A file of photocopiable materials by a poet. This is a valuable resource for any classroom where the teacher hopes to encourage children to be (as Cotton puts it) 'explorers'. Cotton goes on, defiantly in view of the marginalisation of poetry among all the arts, 'We are engaged in no peripheral activity or "frill", this is the real vital stuff of education . . .' This book is notable for, among many things, excellent, sensitive, Ardizzone-like illustrations by the poet and artist, George Szirtes, and the artist, Clarissa Upchurch.

Jill Pirrie (1987) *On Common Ground: A Programme for Teaching Poetry* Hodder and Stoughton

A primer based on Pirrie's children's prize-winning poems from Halesworth Middle School in Suffolk. Introduced by Ted Hughes, this book has a magical quality and some vivid examples of children's writing. It is surer than some books on this subject about the reason why we want children to write poems, as opposed to *how* we get them doing it. This book is about the way we help the child transform the experiences of childhood, first into the notes that betoken involvement with both that experience and the words, and then into a crafted publishable object. In other words, how do we make private celebrations into things that might eventually be public?

Ted Hughes (1967) *Poetry in the Making* Faber

A stimulating and passionate book that speaks eloquently of the centrality of the truth of poetry, and the need children have to search for the truth; of the importance of training the imagination. For crucial quotations from this book, see Hughes's *Winter Pollen: Occasional Prose* ed. William Scammell Faber 1994.

Gervase Phinn (1995) *Touches of Beauty: Teaching Poetry in the Primary School* Roselea Publications

This is a pretty book with some, in my opinion, bad advice. 'Use poems for handwriting practice' seems to me to devalue seriously the learning function of poetry. This is a book of tips of varying quality with rather less rationale than the other books listed here. I include it in this list because it stands for other books of a similar kind. Poetry is not about prettiness, or decorated borders, or handwriting. It is about passion and learning. 'Poetry' (as I've quoted Wallace Stevens as saying) 'is a response to the daily necessity of getting the world right.'

Robert Hull (1988) *Behind the Poem: A Teacher's View of Children Writing* Routledge

This book is now out of print, but secondhand copies are worth buying, because Hull is a vigorous defender of humanistic English teaching. At the centre of the book is an exciting classroom, where groups of children and their poems have been honoured with unpatronising criticism and painstaking labour. These children make notes, talk, draft, talk again, redraft, and share. Some examples:

> The ball is put down so gently that you would think it was made of glass, but it is kicked as if it were hated.

> The sun struck the sign like a single squirt of orange juice on a plate.

Books with a wider reference, but with implications for poetry in the classroom

One book is a touchstone for any serious teacher of English, poetry or otherwise:

Alec Clegg (1964) *The Excitement of Writing* Chatto and Windus

A few quotations from this central text give a clear idea of its drift:

> ... 'creative' writing in schools is neither a luxury allowed by indulgent teachers, nor a form of psychotherapy, but a mode of expression that

children practise readily, deriving confidence and fluency from it . . . It is a fallacy that what can be learned can and must be taught . . . Payers of rates and taxes should note that large sums are spent on textbooks that seem to leave pupils the worse for using them . . .

This all comes from Denys Thompson's trenchant and timeless introduction. The rest of the book is made up of beautiful children's work, and the charismatic Clegg's commentary. This book suggests strongly that the 1960s are less *passé* than is sometimes assumed.

Marie Peel (1967) *Seeing to the Heart* Chatto and Windus
Marjorie L Hourd (1949) *The Education of the Poetic Spirit: A Study in Children's Expression in the English Lesson* Heinemann

Both these are out of date in terms of legislation and prevailing attitudes to the arts. But for anyone who is 'sure of nothing but the truth of the imagination and the holiness of the heart's affections' they are invaluable.

Iona and Peter Opie (1959) *The Lore and Language of Schoolchildren* Oxford University Press

This book enables us as teachers to focus on the roots of children's understanding, their own rhymes. Both scholarly and funny, this book is necessary for anyone who would like to understand children and their relationship to language. I list other books with playground rhymes after this entry.

Iona and Peter Opie (1988) *The Singing Game* Oxford University Press

A rich collection that uses music, texts and photographs to link modern children's games and songs to their forefathers' games and songs all over the world.

Other collections of playground rhymes

Michael Rosen and Susanna Steele (1990) *Inky Pinky Ponky* Collins Lions

Grace Hallworth (1994) *Buy a Penny Ginger and Other Rhymes* Longman

Frank Shaw (1970) *You Know me Aunty Nelly?* Wolfe

Colin Walter (1989) *An Early Start to Poetry* Macdonald

Jennifer Dunn, Nicholas Warburton and Morag Styles (1987) *In Tune with Yourself* Cambridge University Press

This book suggests many ways in which children might write, but it is valuable mostly for the impression it gives of the writers learning as they write, especially about children and their writing. There are not so many books on this subject that admit to being the products of learners as well as teachers that we can afford to ignore examples like this.

Michael Rosen (1981) *I See a Voice* Hutchinson

'I see a voice', says Bottom. Robustly doctrinaire, this book, intended for secondary schools, concentrates the mind wonderfully on humanity and justice.

Ian McMillan (1989) *Against the Grain* Nelson

This book is, in my experience, unique. Made up of idiosyncratic commentary by the poet Ian McMillan, poems, often, as far as I can see, by his friends, and commentary on those poems, it is full of sidelong suggestions for writing. Slangy, trendy, demotic and very good.

Books about writing generally

Sue Thomas (1995) *Creative Writing* University of Nottingham

'A Handbook for Workshop Leaders', this has much for the primary teacher who has become obsessed with children's writing.

Frank Smith (1982) *Writing and the Writer* Heinemann
Donald H Graves (1983) *Writing: Teachers and Children at Work* Heinemann

Neither of these books has much explicitly to do with the teaching of poetry. But if we see poetry in the context of all writing, they are simply necessary. Graves looks closely at what children mean, and at their drafts, and his case studies of teachers working with children in the USA are delightful and enlightening. Smith states profound and dangerous truths, suggesting, for example, that political regimes value reading above writing because we must read to be kept in order, while writing, on the other hand, can change the order. I have much sympathy with this point of view: I think I have presented evidence in this book of children changing the order of things.

Broader Reference

Robin Skelton (1978) *Poetic Truth* Heinemann
Susan Sellers (1991) *Taking Reality by Surprise: Writing for Pleasure and Publication* The Women's Press

'Art must take reality by surprise', said Françoise Sagan, quoted in this book. Intended for women, this book has provided me and (indirectly) many children I've taught with inspirations.

Books on writing and young children (not especially poetry)

Ann Browne (1993) *Helping Children to Write* Paul Chapman

Children emerge as writers. That is a central truth. This book's most powerful sections (and there are many) are about watching that emergence with due attention.

Anne Robinson *et al.* (1990) *Some Day You Will No All About Me: Young Children's Explorations in the World of Letters* Mary Glasgow

Nigel Hall (1989) *Writing with Reason: The Emergence of Authorship in Young Children* Hodder and Stoughton

'Use poems for handwriting practice' seems to me 'to devalue seriously' the learning function of poetry. I wrote that about a book earlier in this list, and this book sums up why. A six-year-old wrote to me once: 'Sasha How light is the sun To Faeb Love from Sasha'. Examples in Hall's book suggest that seeing poetry (or any other kind of writing) as a suitable matter for handwriting practice devalues more than I can say what children have to offer.

Other work of mine on children and poetry

(1992) 'Getting it True: Notes on the Teaching of Poetry' in Booth *et al.* *Curricula for Diversity in Education* Routledge/Open University

(1993) *The Expressive Arts* David Fulton
Chapter 1: 'Six ways of looking at a torch'

In this chapter, I discuss ways of drafting.

(1994)'The Only Lemon in a Bowl of Planets' in Styles *et al. The Prose and the Passion: Children and their Reading* Cassell

(1996) with Dawn Sedgwick *Learning Together* Bloomsbury

One chapter of this book is made up of recently collected rhymes.

Beth's collection of poetry books.

This is necessarily select – and biased towards books written especially for children, as opposed to books written for everyone.

Anthologies

Auden, W H and Garrett, John (1935) *The Poet's Tongue* London: Bell
Avery, Gillian (1994) *The Everyman Anthology of Poetry for Children* London: Everyman
Benson, Gerard (1990) *This Poem Doesn't Rhyme* London: Viking
Causley, Charles (1974) *The Puffin Book of Magic Verse* London: Puffin
Causley, Charles (1978) *The Puffin Book of Salt Sea Verse* London: Puffin
Cotton, John (1996) *I am the Song* London: Nelson
Craft, Ruth (1989) *The Song that Sings the Bird* London: HarperCollins
de la Mare, Walter (1990) *Come Hither* New York: Avenil Press
Harvey, Anne (1985) *Poets in Hand* London: Puffin
Harvey, Anne (1989) *A Puffin Sextet of Poets* London: Puffin
Harvey, Anne (1992) *Occasions: Poems for Every Day and Special Days* London: Puffin
Harvey, Anne (1993) *He Said She Said They Said* London: Blackie
Heaney, Seamus and Hughes, Ted (1982) *The Rattle Bag* London: Faber
McKie, David (1969) *A Flock of Words* London: The Bodley Head
Nicholls, Judith (1993) *Earthways, Earthwise* Oxford: Oxford University Press
Nicholls, Judith (1994) *A Trunkful of Elephants* London: Methuen
Nichols, Grace (1990) *Poetry Jump-Up: Black Poetry* London: Puffin
Owen, Annie (1992) *Pigeons and Other City Poems* London: Macmillan
Rosen, Michael (1985) *The Kingfisher Book of Children's Poetry* London: Kingfisher
Rosen, Michael (1994) *A World of Poetry* London: Kingfisher
Searle, Chris (1983) *Wheel Around the World* London: Macdonald
Sedgwick, Fred (1994) *Collins Primary Poetry* London: HarperCollins
Styles, Morag (1984) *I Like That Stuff* Cambridge: Cambridge University Press
Summerfield, Geoffrey (1970) *Junior Voices* London: Puffin
Townsend, John Rowe (1971) *Modern Poetry* Oxford: Oxford University Press

Individual collections

Agard, John (1990) *Laughter is an Egg* London: Viking
Agard, John and Nichols, Grace (1991) *No Hickory No Dickory No Dock* London: Viking
Berry, James (1990) *When I Dance* London: Puffin
Causley, Charles (1996) *Collected Poems for Children* London: Viking
de la Mare, Walter (1978) *Collected Rhymes and Verses* London: Faber
Dixon, Peter (1988) *Grow Your Own Poems* London: Macmillan
Dixon, Peter (1990) *Big Billy* Winchester: Peter Dixon (Self-publication 30 Cheriton Rd)

Dixon, Peter (1990) *I Heard a Spider Singing* Winchester: Peter Dixon (Self-publication 30 Cheriton Rd)

Dunmore, Helen (1994) *Secrets* London: The Bodley Head

Gowar, Mick (1992) *Carnival of the Animals* London: Viking

Gross, Philip (1989) *Manifold Manor* London: Faber

Mole, John (1979) *Once There Were Dragons* London: Deutsch

Mole, John (1990) *The Mad Parrot's Countdown* Calstock, Cornwall: Peterloo

Mole, John (1992) *The Conjuror's Rabbit* London: Blackie

Silverstein, Shel (1974) *Where the Sidewalk Ends* New York: Harper and Row

Silverstein, Shel (1982) *A Light in the Attic* London: Jonathan Cape

Wright, Kit (1982) *Hot Dog* London: Puffin

Wright, Kit (1987) *Cat Among the Pigeons* London: Puffin

Wright, Kit (1994) *Great Snakes* London: Viking

References

Abbs, Peter (1989) *The Symbolic Order* Lewes: Falmer
Ackroyd, Peter (1984) *T S Eliot* London: Hamish Hamilton
Akhmatova, Anna (1976) *Requiem and Poem Without a Hero* trans. D M Thomas Ohio: Ohio University Press
Auden, W H (1971) *A Commonplace Book* London: Faber
Auden, W H (1976) *Collected Poems* London: Faber
Austen, Jane *Pride and Prejudice* any edition
Bagnall, Nicholas (1973) *New Movements in the Study and Teaching of English* London: Temple Smith
Barthes, Roland (1982) 'On Gide and his Journal', in Susan Sontag (ed.) *A Barthes Reader* London: Cape
Bearne, Eve (ed.) (1995) *Greater Expectations: Children Reading Writing* London: Cassell
Benton, Michael, Teasy, John, Bell, Ray and Hurst, Keith (1988) *Young Readers Responding to Poems* London: Routledge
Booth, Tony, Swann, Will, Masterson, Mary and Potts, Patricia (1992) *Curricula for Diversity in Education* London: Routledge and the Open University
Brownjohn, Sandy (1982) *Does it Have to Rhyme?* London: Hodder and Stoughton
Brownjohn, Sandy (1989) *The Ability to Name Cats* London: Hodder and Stoughton
Bullock, Alan (1975) *A Language for Life* (The Bullock Report) London: HMSO
Carpenter, Humphrey (1981) *W H Auden: A Biography* London: George Allen and Unwin
Chambers, Harry (ed.) (1974) *Phoenix: a poetry magazine.* Philip Larkin Issue
Clegg, Alec (1964) *The Excitement of Writing* London: Chatto and Windus
Coleridge, Samuel Taylor (1907) *Biographica Literaria and Aesthetical Essays* J Shawcross (ed.) Oxford: Oxford University Press
Corbett, Pie and Moses, Brian (1986) *Catapults and Kingfishers: Teaching Poetry in Primary Schools* Oxford: Oxford University Press
Corcoran, Neil (1993) *English Poetry Since 1940* London: Longman
Cotton, John and Sedgwick, Fred (1996) *Two by Two* 52 Melbourne Rd, Ipswich: James Daniel John Press
Crossley-Holland, Kevin (1979) *The Exeter Book Riddles* London: Penguin
Danby, John (1940) *Approach to Poetry* London: Heinemann
Department for Education (undated) *KS3 English Anthology* London: HMSO
Dickinson, Emily (1970) *The Complete Poems* Thomas H. Johnson (ed.) London: Faber
Dowding, John W (1994) 'John Cowper Powys's "Six Precious Words"' *The Powys Review* 29 and 30
Drummond, Mary Jane (1993) *Assessing Children's Learning* London: David Fulton

Duffy, Carol Ann (1993) *Mean Time* London: Anvil

Dunn, Jennifer, Styles, Morag and Warburton, Nick (1987) *In Tune with Yourself* Cambridge: Cambridge University Press

Gibson, J and Wilson, R (1965) *Rhyme and Rhythm Yellow Book* London: Macmillan

Grant, Bill and Harris, Paul (eds) (1991) *The Grizedale Experience: Sculpture, Arts and Theatre in a Lakeland Forest* Edinburgh: Canongate

Gray, Martin (1984) *A Dictionary of Literary Terms* Harlow: Longman

Gray, Richard (1976) *American Poetry of the Twentieth Century* Cambridge: Cambridge University Press

Grigson, Geoffrey (1982) *The Private Art* London: Allison and Busby

Hawkes, Terence (1977) *Structuralism and Semiotics* London: Methuen

Heaney, Seamus (1979) *Field Work* London: Faber

Hemingway, Ernest (1935) *A Farewell to Arms* London: Penguin

Holbrook, David (1961) *English for Maturity* Cambridge: Cambridge University Press

Holbrook, David (1964) *The Secret Places* Cambridge: Cambridge University Press

Holbrook, David 1969) *Children's Writing* Cambridge: Cambridge University Press

Holmes, Richard (1989) *Coleridge: Early Visions* London: Penguin

Holub, Miroslav (1985) 'Miroslav Holub interviewed by Dennis O'Driscoll' *Poetry Review* Volume 75 Number 3

Hopkins, Gerard Manley (1948) *Collected Poems* Robert Bridges (ed.) Enlarged by W H Gardner Oxford: Oxford University Press

Hourd, Marjorie L (1949) *The Education of the Poetic Spirit* London: Heinemann

Hull, Robert (1988) *Behind the Poem: A Teacher's View of Children Writing* London: Routledge

Jonson, Ben (1975) *Collected Poems* Oxford: Oxford University Press

Joyce, James *Ulysses* any edition

Langdon, Margaret (1961) *Let the Children Write – An Explanation of Intensive Writing* London: Longman

Larkin, Philip (1974) 'Worksheets of "At Grass"' in Chambers (1974)

Larkin, Philip (1988) *Collected Poems* London: Marvell Press/Faber

Lindop, Grevel (1981) *The Opium Eater* London: Dent

McNeill, Helen (1986) *Emily Dickinson* London: Virago

MacShane, Frank (1973) 'Borges on poetry' in J. Robson (ed.) *Poetry Dimension* London: Abacus

Magee, Wes (1988) *Morning Break* Cambridge: Cambridge University Press

Mandelstam, Osip (1981) *Osip Mandelstam's Stone* Robert Tracy (trans. and ed.) Princeton University Press

Morgan, Edwin (1982) *Poems of Thirty Years* Manchester: Carcanet

National Curriculum (1995) London: HMSO

Panichas, George A (ed.) (1977) *The Simone Weil Reader* New York: David McKay

Peel, Marie (1967) *Seeing to the Heart* London: Chatto

Pirrie, Jill (1987) *On Common Ground* London: Hodder and Stoughton

Raine, Craig (1979) *A Martian Sends a Postcard Home* Milton Keynes: Open University Press

Robson, Jeremy (1973) *Poetry Dimension 1* London: Abacus

Rogers, Carl (1970) *On Becoming a Person: A Therapist's View of Psychotherapy* Boston: Houghton Mifflin

Rogers, Timothy (ed.) (1979) *Those First Affections* London: Routledge

Scannell, Vernon (1977) *A Proper Gentleman* London: Robson

Sedgwick, Fred (1988) 'The Sifter's Story' *Cambridge Journal of Education* Volume 18 Number 1

Sedgwick, Fred (1989) *Here Comes the Assembly Man* London: Falmer
Sedgwick, Fred (1992) *The Expressive Arts* London: David Fulton
Sedgwick, Fred (1994a) *Advice* (Collins Primary Poetry No. 4) London: HarperCollins
Sedgwick, Fred (1994b) *Personal, Social and Moral Education* London: David Fulton
Sedgwick, Dawn and Sedgwick, Fred (1993) *Drawing to Learn* London: Hodder and Stoughton
Sedgwick, Dawn and Sedgwick, Fred (1996a) *Art Across the Curriculum* London: Hodder and Stoughton
Sedgwick, Dawn and Sedgwick, Fred (1996b) *Learning Together: Enhance your Child's Creativity* London: Bloomsbury
Shakespeare, William (1963) *The Sonnets* Martin Seymour-Smith (ed.) London: Heinemann
Shakespeare[1], William (1966) *The Sonnets* John Dover Wilson (ed.) Cambridge: Cambridge University Press
Skelton, Robin (1978) *Poetic Truth* London: Heinemann
Smith, Frank (1982) *Writing and the Writer* London: Heinemann
Sontag, Susan (ed.) (1982) *A Barthes Reader* London: Cape
Spencer, Herbert (1929) *Education* London: Watts
Stenhouse, Lawrence (1976) *An Introduction to Curriculum Design and Development* London: Heinemann
Stephens, Meic (1990) *Dictionary of Literary Quotations* London: Routledge
Stillman, Frances (1966) *The Poet's Manual and Rhyming Dictionary* London: Thames and Hudson
Styles, Morag, Bearne, Eve and Watson, Victor (1992) *After Alice: Exploring Children's Literature* London: Cassell
Styles, Morag, Bearne, Eve and Watson, Victor (1994) *The Prose and the Passion: Children and their Reading* London: Cassell
Styles, Morag and Drummond, Mary Jane (eds) (1993) *The Politics of Reading* Cambridge: University of Cambridge and Homerton College
Summerfield, Geoffrey (1970) *Junior Voices, the Fourth Book* London: Penguin
Thomas, Edward (1936) *Collected Poems* London: Faber
Thompson, Denys (ed.) (1969) *Directions in the Teaching of English* Cambridge: Cambridge University Press
Vernon, P E (1970) *Creativity* London: Penguin
Weil, Simone (1977) *Reader* George A. Panichas (ed.) New York: David McKay
Willans, Geoffrey and Searle, Ronald (1958) *Down with Skool!* London: Max Parrish
Wright , David (1965) *English Poetry 1940–60* London: Penguin
Yeats, W B (1950) *Collected Poems* London: Macmillan

[1] I refer to other works by Shakespeare, but have not referred to them here again because they are familiar, and because my references are not restricted to particular editions. Similarly, I have not included Bible references.

Index